MURDEROUS MINDS SOVIET UNION

MURDEROUS MINDS SOVIET UNION

International Serial Killers Encyclopedia
Book 2

ALAN R. WARREN

House of Mystery Publishing

Seattle, Washington, USA

Vancouver, British Columbia, Canada

First Edition

ISBN (Paperback): 978-1-989980-36-1
ISBN (eBook): 978-1-989980-37-8

Cover design, formatting, layout, and editing by Evening Sky Publishing Services

Contents

Book Description

Step into the abyss with this gripping series that unravels the chilling tales of serial killers worldwide. From the damp and foggy streets of Victorian London to the bustling metropolises of modern-day America, no corner of the globe is left unexplored. Each book in the series delves into a different region, offering a comprehensive look at the infamous serial killers who have left a trail of terror in their wake.

The *International Serial Killers Encyclopedia* series sheds light on the murderous minds of many killers, including their motivations, methods, and madness, through detailed research and explicit retelling of events. Some are notorious names that echo through history books, while others are lesser-known killers whose stories are no less harrowing. Each volume reveals a new layer of darkness.

Amidst the horror, there are tales of resilience and justice – the strength of survivors and the justice meted out by the tireless efforts of law enforcement. These stories are a compelling blend of true crime facts and psychological insight and a haunting journey through the twisted minds and deeds of serial killers from around the world. Prepare to be enthralled, horrified, and captivated as you delve into the shadows of the abyss.

Volume 2 of the *International Serial Killers Encyclopedia* series focuses on the most notorious serial killers from the Soviet Union Era of history. In the shadows of the Iron Curtain, amidst the turmoil of revolution and the rigid structures of the Soviet regime, a different kind of darkness lurked. Behind closed doors and beneath the watchful eyes of the state, a breed of killers emerged, their crimes shrouded in secrecy and fear from the haunting corridors of Moscow to the desolate landscapes of Siberia.

From Andrei Chikatilo, a.k.a. the "Butcher of

Rostov," whose insatiable hunger for violence claimed the lives of dozens, leaving a trail of mutilation and terror in his wake, to Vasili Komaroff, a.k.a. the "Wolf of Moscow," who killed so many men, he couldn't even remember his kill count. Each chapter reveals the brutal tales of individuals consumed by their darkest desires and a compelling blend of true crime and psychological intrigue.

Murderous Minds Soviet Union delves deeper, revealing the many enigmatic figures who haunted a nation's collective consciousness. Each chapter unveils a new layer of horror and intrigue where the echoes of the past continue to reverberate to this day.

Introduction

In this exploration of the macabre, we journey through the clandestine corridors of Soviet society, where the screams of the innocent drown out the echoes of footsteps. From the bustling streets of Moscow to the frozen expanses of Siberia, each chapter unveils a new layer of horror, a new face of evil.

The Soviet Union, with its vast expanse and diverse population, became a breeding ground for the darkest impulses of humanity. Within its borders, the likes of Andrei Chikatilo, the "Butcher of Rostov," roamed freely, preying upon the vulnerable with impunity. His gruesome acts of violence and depravity shocked the world, leaving a scar on the collective consciousness that still lingers to this day.

But Chikatilo was not alone. *Murderous Minds Soviet Union* delves deeper, uncovering the stories of "The Leningrad Strangler," "The Bloody Casanova," and myriad other twisted individuals whose names are etched into the annals of infamy. Through meticulous research and vivid storytelling, we confront the chilling reality of their crimes, exploring the motivations, methods, and madness that drove them to commit unspeakable acts.

Yet, amidst the darkness, there are also glimpses of light. This book bears witness to the resilience of the human spirit, the bravery of those who fought against injustice, and the triumph of good over evil. Through the tireless efforts of law enforcement, the courage of survivors, and the determination of ordinary citizens, justice was served, and the shadows were pushed back, if only for a moment.

As we embark on this harrowing journey through the depths of Soviet society, we are reminded that evil knows no bounds and that serial killers can thrive even in the most unlikely of places. But we are also reminded of the power of truth, justice, and the enduring human spirit that refuses to be extinguished, even in the face of unspeakable horror.

ONE

Vasili Komaroff

WOLF OF MOSCOW

Vasili Komaroff was born Vasily Terentyevich Petrov in Vitebsk Governorate, Soviet Union, in January 1871. His family was poor, and he was one of fifteen children. His father was a heavy drinker and would often make his sons drink with him, which, for Vasili, started at the age of fifteen.

When Vasili reached the age of nineteen, he was conscripted into the army and served for four years. At the age of twenty-eight, Vasili was married. During the Russian-Japanese War in 1904, he traveled to fight for the army. While away from home, he started to make money from robberies and thefts. He was arrested for stealing from a military warehouse and sentenced to serve one year in prison. During that year, his wife died from cholera during an outbreak.

Once Vasili was released from jail, he moved to Riga, now known as Latvia. He met and married a Polish woman, Sophia, and they would have two children. As an adult, Vasili continued drinking and was now an alcoholic. But unlike his father, he was a mean drunk. After drinking, Vasili would always end up fighting with Sophia and beating her. Often, if the kids were awake, he would beat them as well.

When the Germans invaded the Baltics in World War I, Vasili took his family and fled to Volga. Two years later, when the citizens began to revolt against the government, he joined the Red Army and, over time, became a platoon leader.

During the revolution, he was captured in one of the battles. Vasili managed to escape and was never tried by the Russian Revolutionary Tribune.

When Vasili returned home, he changed his name to Vasili Ivanovich Komaroff to avoid being arrested. Later, in 1920, he moved to Moscow with his family. He got a job as a "carriage driver," another name for a horse racer. Horse racing as a competitive sport was quite popular in Britain, where a single horse pulled a much larger carriage during the race. Vasili also dabbled in minor crimes, such as petty thefts.

In 1921, under Vladimir Lenin's rule, the Soviet Union allowed its citizens to own their businesses and make a profit. Komaroff decided to become a horse trader to make money. However, it was pretty much a ruse to lure his victims. Komaroff would meet a potential customer and invite them to his home, where he would serve them vodka and food. During the night, he would kill them by hitting them over the head with a hammer or cutting their throats with a knife. He would put their body into a large bag and hide it in the house so that his wife or kids wouldn't discover it. Then, when he had the chance, he would take the bag with the dead body and either dump it into the Moscow River or bury it in the ground.

Later that year, Komaroff's wife accidentally discovered one of the men he had murdered hidden in a bag at the house. Sophia wasn't upset or angry about him killing another man. She decided that she would help him to commit more murders. Over the next two years, the couple would murder at least twenty-nine people.

Police discovered some of the bodies of the men that Komaroff had murdered, and they started what turned into a two-year investigation. Twenty-one men's corpses were recovered. All of the men he murdered were involved in the buying and selling of horses, so police began canvassing people who were involved in the business of horse trading. During their interviews, they heard about Komaroff always having a new horse to sell, usually twice a week. Komaroff was seen leaving with a potential customer, and that customer always disappeared and was never seen again.

In February 1923, police visited Komaroff's home to question him. While there, they found the remains of a man partially covered by a stack of hay. Somehow, Komaroff escaped arrest that day, but in March, he was found in a distant town, arrested, and returned to Moscow.

During his interrogation by police, Komaroff admitted to murdering thirty-three men. He added that he might have killed more, but he just couldn't remember. His motive was strictly to steal their horse and/or their money.

Later, Komaroff brought the police to the locations where he had disposed of his victims. Another six bodies were recovered. Police also arrested his wife, Sophia, and charged her with the murders as well. They figured that with the amount of men he killed and the tiny house they lived in, there was no way she couldn't have known that he was killing these men.

Both Vasili and Sophia were convicted of thirty-three murders and sentenced to death. The couple was shot by a firing squad in Moscow on June 18, 1923.

TWO

Alexander Labutkin

THE ONE-ARM BANDIT

Alexander Alekseevich Labutkin was born in St. Petersburg, Soviet Union, in 1910. The exact date of his birth is not known. In 1928, he got a job as a gunsmith and worked for the Krasnoznamyonets Arms Factory. His employer was working on creating a replacement for gunpowder with gun cotton at the time. In 1930, when Labutkin was working in the woods, taking stumps out of the ground using an explosive, he accidentally got caught in one of the explosions and lost his right hand.

Labutkin had to change jobs because he couldn't continue working as a gunsmith with only one hand, so he worked as a steam conductor in Leningrad. Labutkin was known to have an ego, and he felt that this new job was an embarrassment. He often dressed in the most expensive suits and hats and spoke in a sophisticated manner.

On August 30, 1933, Labutkin, disguised as a mushroom picker, walked through the woods behind the old powder plant where he worked. During his walk, he ran into two men and three women who were also walking in the woods. He pulled out his gun and began shooting at them. Both men and two of the women died there. One of the women survived and, when found, was taken to the hospital. Sadly, she died later that day in the hospital.

Four months later, on December 2, 1933, two more men were shot in the same wooded area. Both men's footwear was stolen from their corpses.

They had been murdered with the same type of bullets as the five others back in August.

The following year, on April 11th, Labutkin surprised a locksmith walking home from work. Labutkin shot the man and stole the money he was carrying, a suitcase, and even some of his teeth, which had gold in them.

Labutkin wouldn't strike again for six months. On November 13, 1934, he came across a birdwatcher who was out viewing birds in the park. All he stole from that man was a birdcage.

The following year, 1935, Labutkin went into the woods again to look for victims. In the two hours he was there, he ran into two married couples who had just been out for a walk in the park after dinner. He ended up shooting both couples to death and stole nothing.

In February, he shot and killed a single man who was in the park having his lunch. In March, he attempted to kill another couple who was out for a walk in the park, but the woman survived and was taken to the hospital. She was able to identify Labutkin as the gunman, and he was arrested shortly after.

During the police's interrogation of Labutkin, he confessed to committing twelve murders, and during his trial in July 1935, he was found guilty and sentenced to death. He was executed by firing squad.

Labutkin's wife was also arrested as an accomplice to the murders and for concealing her husband's crimes. She, too, was convicted but given a prison sentence of thirty-five years.

THREE

Vladimir Vinnichevsky

THE URALS MONSTER

Vladimir Georgeievich Vinnichevsky was born in Varkhnyaya Saida, Sverdlovsk Oblast, Soviet Union, on June 8, 1923. His father was a crew chief for the town utility company, and his mother was an accountant. Financially, his family was on the higher end of the average family in the Soviet Union at that time. They even had their own house.

Vladimir grew up two houses away from the famous sculptor Ernst Neizvastny. The two were in the same grade throughout school, except in the sixth grade when Vladimir failed and had to repeat the grade. Years later, after Vladimir was arrested and charged with murders, Neizvastny told the police and court that Vladimir was timid, quiet, and liked to spend a lot of his time alone. He also said that often, Vladimir went to the bathroom and was in there for hours. Neizvastny said that Vladimir didn't seem to have any desire for girls and that he admitted he didn't want to have sex with them.

The first murder that police uncovered was that of a four-year-old girl, Gerta Grebanova, who was playing in her family's front yard by herself in late September 1938. Vladimir, who was fifteen years old at the time, walked through the gate of their front yard and lured the child into the family's backyard garden. There, he strangled her until she passed out. He then pulled a knife out of his jacket and stabbed her several times in her head. He only stopped stabbing her when his knife got stuck in her skull. When he tried to remove it, the knife broke.

When police found Gerta's body, they removed her head and kept it as evidence because it still had some of the murderer's knife embedded in it. They reasoned that when the murderer used the knife again, they would be able to prove it was the same killer responsible. Instead, after Vladimir murdered Greta and broke his knife, he threw the rest of it away in his neighbor's garbage and began using a screwdriver to kill his victims.

Vladimir murdered both boys and girls. And not only in his hometown of Sverdlovsk but also in neighboring towns such as Nizhny Tagi and Kushva. He intended to throw the investigators off the trail by murdering children in other locations.

At first, Vladimir began to attack young girls to try and have intercourse with them. After the first few attempts didn't work because he was too large for the girls, he started to perform anal sex on them. He figured out that this would work on young boys as well. Vladimir went on to attack, rape, and murder several children until the Fall of 1939.

On October 24, 1939, three-year-old Vyacheslav Volkov was placed outside the family's front door to play while his mother was getting ready to go shopping. Vladimir happened to walk by their house, saw the boy, entered the front gate, grabbed the boy, and ran. The boy's mother heard a commotion, went outside, and screamed. Vladimir quickly jumped on a tram with the boy and got away. Three high school cadet police were patrolling the tram when they saw Vladimir jump on with the boy. They decided to follow Vladimir, who got off the tram near a wooded area, and three of them followed. Vladimir took the boy into the woods, and once he found a clearing, he removed his scarf and began to strangle the boy. The three cadets found him, stopped him from choking the boy, and placed him under arrest.

During the detective's interrogation of Vladimir, he readily confessed to the murders. He even kept a list of his murders at home. He had encrypted the list in case someone had come across it so they couldn't understand it. The list was brought out during the trial and shown as an exhibit. At the trial, Vladimir's parents stated that they denounced their son.

On April 8, 1935, the courts in the Soviet Union adopted a new resolution to impose the death penalty on all citizens from the age of twelve in an attempt to try and bring down the number of juvenile criminals in the country. Before that, the death penalty was only handed down to adults, which was considered to be when a person reached the age of nineteen.

On January 16, 1940, Vladimir Vinnichevsky was convicted of eight murders and sentenced to death. He filed an appeal to be released to fight in World War II, but it was denied. He was executed by firing squad at the age of seventeen. In the Soviet Union at this time, they never returned the bodies of the executed criminals to their families. Instead, they would bury them in an unknown place somewhere near Moscow.

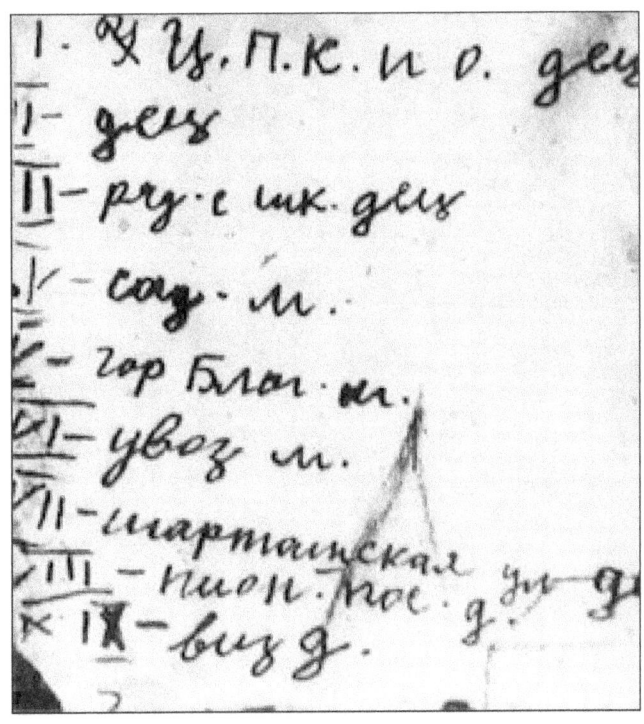

FOUR

Philipp Tyurin

THE HELLRAISER

Philipp Petrovich Tyurin was born in Sumerki, Ryazan Governorate, Soviet Union, in the year 1910. The exact date or location is unknown. In fact, not much is known about Tyurin's childhood or family before World War II. Tyurin's first record was when he fought in the War and was seriously wounded. He was treated at the military hospital located in Leningrad.

When the war ended, Tyurin got a job working in the canteen of a Bolshevik truck plant. Being a teamster, he was also given a room to live in at the plant and a horse-drawn carriage to use whenever needed. He lived there until he was arrested in 1947.

Tyurin would go to the local markets where people traded and bought everything from food to clothing. He would look for people who seemed to have a lot of items or money. Tyurin would tell his intended victims that he could sell them or trade them for potatoes at a very cheap price. They would agree and follow him to his room. Once they were in his room, he would explain that the potatoes were in the cellar and ask them to go down and gather them for themselves. He said that he would follow them down to help them. But once the customer headed down the stairs, he would follow them and hit them over the head with a heavy item.

Later, though, during the police investigation, they were unable to find any traces of blood from an attack or anything else to show that a person had been killed on the stairs. Detectives figured that Tyurin must have killed his victims outside of the room.

Tyurin confessed to having murdered twenty-nine people between April 1945 and December 1946. Most of his victims' remains were never found, likely because Tyurin dumped several of his victims in the Utkina Zavod – a nearby boatyard on the riverbank.

In December 1946, two bodies were discovered behind the room where Tyurin had been living. Police searched all the surrounding buildings and found traces of blood on the walls of his room. Upon analysis of the blood, they discovered that it belonged to animals. But it was too late. The detectives had their sights set on Tyurin.

After police arrested Tyurin and he made his confessions, they were able to locate the remains of thirteen of his victims. Several of his victims were not found, but in the end, the police charged Tyurin with fourteen murders. He was convicted and sentenced to death by firing squad. Tyurin was executed on May 4, 1947.

FIVE

Boris Gusakov

B oris Vasilyevich Gusakov was born in Balashikha, Moscow, on January 1, 1938. At the age of three, Gusakov witnessed a bomb explode, which killed several Germans, including a girl whose head was blown off right in front of him. He was traumatized by what he saw, but no treatment was available to him because of the ongoing world war. His family were all heavy drinkers and never cared for him much.

After finishing school in 1955, he got a job as a photographer, married a librarian, and had a daughter in 1958. Shortly after that, Gusakov started his service in the army, which lasted three years, before being discharged after he was convicted of theft.

Gusakov went back home in May 1962 and returned to being a photographer for the Kartolitografi Factory. While he worked there, he committed his first known attack on a girl who was in the Moscow Library in December 1963. He couldn't control his victim enough to stop her from screaming and attracting attention, and she escaped. But he escaped capture as well. At the time, police blamed the attack on a known Moscow killer of the time, Vladimir Lonesyan.

Gusakov's second attack and first murder took place at Tomilinsky Park six months later, on June 21, 1964, when he attacked, sexually assaulted, and killed eleven-year-old Valya Scherbakova.

In August 1965, Gusakov got a new job working for the Ministry of Internal Affairs in the laboratory of film and photos. Within a month of getting that job, he raped and killed another student at the same park.

In 1967, Gusakov became a photographic engineer at a chemical research plant. During his employment there, he lured two first-year college students into the attic of the plant, where he raped and killed both of them. He even left the murder weapon, a water pipe, with their bodies, which had his fingerprints on it.

When police discovered the two bodies and the murder weapon, they were also able to lift the fingerprints off it. The girl's classmates reported that the last person they were seen with was a student named Oleg Ryabok. When they compared the prints they got from the pipe, they didn't match.

In April 1968, in Lyuberetsky District, Gusakov murdered a nine-year-old girl. During that attack, he was interrupted by a couple, so he started to assault them with a rock. He ended up killing the woman, but the man survived and later gave a good description of their assailant. Through further investigation, police were able to link the crime with the previous murders of the two students.

On May 16, 1968, two tenth-grade girls agreed to meet Gusakov for a walk in the park.

Once they met, Gusakov gave them drinks he had poisoned earlier. But he must have done something wrong as the poison didn't work. Shortly after they started walking through the woods, he pulled a meat cleaver from his bag and swung it at them. Both girls began to yell and run. Just then, a police officer patrolling the park heard them and came running. Gusakov was arrested.

The following year, in 1969, Gusakov was tried and convicted of five murders and sentenced to death. In the early Summer of 1970, Gusakov was executed by firing squad in Moscow.

SIX

Anatoly Slivko

Anatoly Yemelianovich Slivko was born in Izerbash, Dagestan ASSR, USSR, on December 28, 1938. He was the oldest of two children who lived with both parents in poverty. At the time, Ukraine was experiencing a famine, and his father was an alcoholic who constantly fought with his mother in front of the kids. Slivko was often ill and very much a loner.

After the Soviets entered World War II, Slivko's father was conscripted into the Red Army and sent away for battle. At home, Slivko and his remaining family dealt with the continuous bombings by Germans. In 1943, Slivko and his family had to run away from their home once the Germans had invaded it. Often, the children of his neighborhood had to hide in the local cemetery to avoid capture.

As Slivko reached his teenage years, he realized that he was homosexual, which embarrassed him. He believed it was wrong, so he kept it a secret from everyone else. He also figured that he had issues with what would be called erectile dysfunction in today's time.

Slivko desperately wanted to leave his home and escape his town. After graduating from high school in 1956, he applied to the University of Moscow but failed the entrance exam. After that setback, he decided to begin compulsory military service, where he was sent to the Far East. Slivko always appeared passive and often wouldn't look people directly in the eyes, which caused the other trainees in the military to make fun of him. By 1960, his superior officers decided that Slivko was not meant for the army and gave him an early discharge for health reasons.

After that, Slivko moved to Stavropol Krai and got a job as a telephone engineer. He allowed his younger sister to live with him there until she got herself a job. She soon started working in a factory and moved out on her own. During this time, Slivko's sister introduced him to a coworker from the factory, Lyudmila. Slivko began to date Lyudmila, and they got married the following year, in 1963. After their marriage, the couple moved to Nevinnomyssk. Later, during Slivko's interrogations with detectives, he would tell them that during their seventeen-year marriage, the couple only had intercourse ten times. After the birth of their second child, they never had sex again.

One evening in 1961, while returning home from his work, Slivko witnessed a traffic accident where a drunk motorcyclist drove off the road onto a sidewalk and struck and killed a teenage boy. Later, Slivko admitted to being sexually excited by the accident and having what he called a powerful orgasm while he watched it. He explained that he would get excited each time he thought about the boy convulsing, shaking, and moaning. Watching the boy die was a pivotal moment in his life. He said it was at that moment that he realized he had the desire to have sex with other young men.

A few months after witnessing the accident, Slivko started a young men's club. It was a place for young men to form friendships and engage in activities with other young men, a place to take them off the street and keep them from getting into trouble. Even though the intention sounded good, Slivko had his reasons for having the club.

One year after it started, one of the boys who frequented there burned the building. The young man was angry with Slivko. It was unknown why, but no charges were ever filed against him.

Slivko found a new location to house the boys' club closer to his home than the original club. The club continued to be a good thing in the public eye, and people around town appreciated having it. The boys' parents liked all the activities the boys had in the club, and it kept them from getting into trouble. Slivko regularly went on several-day hiking and mountain climbing trips with the boys. The local press frequently mentioned Slivko and the club, which even received an award from the communist party for contributing to educating young men and boys.

Over time, Slivko became very popular among

the citizens and was regularly on the radio. By 1977, Slivko ran and was elected Deputy of the City Council. Also that year, Slivko was awarded the Honored Teacher of the Soviet Union award.

In the Summer of 1963, Slivko desperately wanted to relive the witnessing of the accident. For him to relive his sexual fantasy, he would select a boy between the ages of eleven and fifteen, who was the same age as the boy who died in the crash, and tell them that he wanted to make a movie. The film would reenact a scene where a Nazi soldier hung a boy. He set up practice runs of the hanging to gain the boy's confidence. On each practice run, he was gentle and assured the boy that he would revive him from being unconscious after filming the scene.

Slivko had bought a schoolboy's uniform and shoes for them to wear during the filming, and after they were dressed, he put them to sleep by inhaling ether. Once the boy was passed out, he tied the noose around their neck and then took their clothing off them. Slivko arranged the boy's bodies in different positions, molested them, and masturbated over them. Slivko filmed much of it with his 16mm film camera. He had gained the confidence of the boy's parents by telling them that he was making educational films for the kids to watch to learn about how evil the Nazis were to them during the War. Slivko later used these films to relive his sexual fantasies.

In the following twenty-two years, Slivko convinced forty-three boys to be in a film. In thirty-six cases, he sexually assaulted the boys and masturbated about them. After he was done filming the boys, he helped them regain consciousness, and they did not remember what had happened to them during the time they passed out. However, in the other seven films, Slivko went much further on the remaining boys. He lost control and murdered them after molesting them. He then dismembered the bodies, burned them, and later disposed of the remains. He kept their shoes as a trophy to relive the fantasy later when he watched the film.

Fifteen-year-old Nikolai Dobryshev was Slivko's first known victim on June 2, 1964. He later claimed that he killed the boy by accident because he was unable to revive him after filming the scene. He further claimed that he went into panic mode and decided to take apart the boy's body, burn the remains, and dump him into the Kuban River. Slivko also burned the film and pictures he had taken while with Dobryshev but kept his shoes.

Slivko's second known murder happened in May 1965 after Aleksei Kovalenko came to his club. In this case, Slivko killed the boy intentionally, keeping the film of his molestation of the boy and the boy's shoes as trophies. Slivko also burned Kovalenko's body and dumped it into the river.

Slivko also killed fifteen-year-old Aleksandr Nesmeyanov on November 14, 1973. While searching for the missing boy, the police went to the club and talked with Slivko since the boy was a member. Slivko helped with some of the group searches to try to find the boy. He became part of the searches for missing boys to try and sway the searches from the actual locations where he dumped the bodies.

Another victim, Andrei Pogasyan, was eleven years old when Slivko killed him. He was also a member of Slivko's boys club when he went missing on May 11, 1975. He was last seen leaving for the club to film a movie with Slivko. Police questioned Slivko at his club and dismissed him as a possible suspect after a few minutes.

Sergey Fatniev became Slivko's fifth murder victim in 1980. Slivko had rearranged the boy's body several times during the filming and sexual assault of the boy.

Slivko killed another boy, Vyacheslav Khvisik, at the age of fifteen in the Fall of 1984. Not much is known about this murder except that Slivko had kept a written record of it.

Slivko's seventh and final murder victim on July 23, 1985, was thirteen-year-old Sergey Pavlov. He also went missing after leaving his home to make a film at the boy's club he belonged to. Police investigated and found nothing, so they considered the boy a runaway. Pavlov's parents didn't believe he had run away, so they searched and questioned people. They uncovered disturbing details about the films the boys were making, especially the fact that, often, the boys passed out while making the films. So Pavlov's parents went to a prosecutor, Tamara Languyeva, and asked her to start an investigation.

Languyeva spoke with several of Slivko's club members and learned that all the missing boys were members of the club and were last seen going to the club to make a movie with Slivko. She also learned that all the boys who were part of the films had passed out during the filming.

Languyeva searched Slivko's property and club in December 1985. During the search, police located a locked dark room in the basement. It was there that the police found several photographs and films that showed the boys being sexually assaulted, murdered, and dismembered. They also found all the shoes that Slivko had taken from the boys. The murder weapons that he used in the films—knives, axes, ropes, and a rubber hose—were also discovered in his dark room.

Slivko was arrested and taken to jail. He confessed to the seven murders once he realized that the police had discovered all the films and pictures. Slivko claimed that he knew he had an issue with his sexual fantasies and could only keep it under control by killing the seven boys and filming the murder so that he could watch the films later to relieve his desire to kill others.

Slivko took police to where six of his murder victims had been dumped, but his first victim was not where he said it was and was never located. In March 1986, Slivko was charged with seven murders, seven counts of sexual assault, and seven counts of necrophilia.

Slivko's trial started in June 1986, where he pleaded guilty to all charges, his defense being that the murders were all accidental, not intentional. Slivko was found guilty on all charges and sentenced to death. Slivko filed two different appeals for the death sentence, but both were rejected.

Before Slivko was executed, he agreed to try and help the police solve another murder case that was going on, the "Forest Strip Killer." Detectives wanted to try and find out what kinds of things go through the minds of serial murderers. Slivko told them that if he had been able to accept his sexual perversion, being homosexual, he might have been able to get help from a doctor, and they might have been able to solve his problem. The detectives who interviewed Slivko about the unknown serial killer later conveyed that the information they received from Slivko was not helpful and most of it was wrong.

Slivko was executed by a single bullet in the back of his head in a soundproofed cell on September 16, 1989.

SEVEN

Vasily Filippenko

THE LENINGRAD STRANGLER

V asily Efimovich Filippenko was born in
Kerch, Crimean ASSR—an autonomous
Soviet Socialist Republic government
within the Soviet Union—in 1936. He lived there
for the first thirty years of his life. Not much is

known about his birth and childhood. In fact, he was relatively unknown until injuring himself while working as a crane operator in a port. He fell from a great height, which caused him seventeen broken bones.

During his treatment, his wife divorced him, fearing that he would be disabled for the rest of his life. Filippenko was left angry at his wife for such a betrayal, and his anger grew into a deep hostility towards women in general.

When Filippenko recovered, he decided to start over. In 1966, he moved to Leningrad and returned to work as a crane operator there. He also became part of the voluntary People's Druzhina, a group of citizens who went out on patrol to try to stop crimes.

The following year, Filippenko began attacking different women he came across in the Obvodny Canal area of Leningrad. He would walk around watching people on the streets, and whenever he saw a woman who parted ways from a man, he would follow her and, if he could, make her his victim.

During the overnight hours of May 23, 1967, he spotted nineteen-year-old Nina Petukhova, who walked with a sailor until they reached the canal. There, the two separated, and Filippenko followed her. He approached her, and the two began to chat. Once they reached the women's hostel, where Petukhova lived, she said goodbye and turned to walk in. He quickly grabbed her from behind and dragged her into some bush, where he beat, sexually assaulted, and strangled her to death.

Later, he would testify that she had suddenly reminded him of his ex-wife, and that's why he attacked her. When her body was discovered, police noticed semen on her and were able to get the attacker's blood type. They would also find two of his hairs gripped in her hand.

Initially, detectives believed the suspect in Petukhova's attack and murder was the sailor Sergei Sergeyev, whom she had met earlier that same evening. The police contacted the ship he was stationed on and told the commander they needed to question him. Sergeyev was placed in solitary until the police arrived and escorted him back to headquarters. The police soon got the results from the hair sample and blood type, and neither was a match for Sergeyev, so he was released.

The next attack occurred in July of that same year and near the location of the previous one. He had beaten the unnamed victim before strangling her until she passed out. Then, he raped her. In this case, and for no apparent reason, Filippenko left his victim alive.

Police were called, and the girl was taken to the hospital. There, she mistakingly identified her attacker as twenty-four-year-old Igor Vorobyev after looking at photos of previously convicted felons who lived in the area. Vorobyev's blood type matched the blood type of the attacker and of Nina Petukhova's murderer, but his hair sample didn't match. Regardless, the police arrested Vorobyev for the rape of the second victim but not for the Petukhova murder.

Before his trial began in September 1967, a university student was arrested for raping and trying to strangle another woman in Lenin Park. They tried to link the student to the other two attacks, but his blood and hair didn't match those recovered from the crime scene in the Petukhova murder. The police had the student stand in a lineup for the second attack victim who survived. This time, she chose this suspect as her attacker, which meant that she had identified two different men as her attacker. Since the defense would have access to her conflicting accusations, they didn't feel the case would be strong enough to take to court. It was later discovered that this victim had myopia and never wore glasses.

Even though there would be two more murders before Vorobyev's trial started in November, and even with the testimony of witnesses, including Vorobyev's wife, claiming that he was at home at the time of the attack, he was still convicted and sentenced to six years in prison.

The next murder committed by Filippenko was when twenty-five-year-old Tatyana Kuznetsova, a night shift nurse at the Botkin Hospital, was taking her break outside in a courtyard. At the same time, Filippenko was following another nurse around the hospital, waiting for his chance to attack her. Somehow, he lost that nurse during his pursuit and ended up in the courtyard. Filippenko then attacked, raped, and strangled Kuznetsova. But unlike his previous victims, he stole her money as well.

On the morning of October 18th, Leningrad had a flood through its downtown core, causing most residents to evacuate the area. That night, Filippenko found Galina Ivanova on an embankment overlooking the river. He then attacked her and dragged her to an abandoned construction site, where he raped and killed her.

Police began to hold information from the

press to help them separate good tips from bad ones they received daily from people. They also started a live bait operation where they had undercover female officers hang around the downtown river area, hoping to lure the attacker, but they had no success.

Even with all of this happening, Filippenko would kill again and near the canal in the same area as he had attacked before. His next victim was a nineteen-year-old university student, Faina Anchak, who he strangled until she passed out, and then he raped her. He later admitted to thinking he had left Faina alive. He didn't realize it, but when he strangled her, he broke her hyoid bone, and after her trachea swelled, she died from suffocation.

After this attack and murder, the communist party leadership came down hard on the city police. They doubled the undercover plants and made it so that there were dozens of police patrolling the area every day and at every hour. There was never supposed to be a time when you couldn't see at least a dozen officers walking the streets in that area.

With the amount of pressure that was now on police to catch the attacker, they were arresting anyone who even said something wrong or rude to any woman on the street. One person they arrested was Viktor Danilov, twenty-six years old, who was caught touching, caressing, and swearing at a woman. Danilov was what people referred to as a "golden youth" because his parents had good jobs and were influential in the ruling party. They had to release him but decided to keep him under surveillance.

Three days later, after Danilov committed another minor assault on a woman, police detained him and searched his apartment. There, they found several pornographic magazines and hair curlers that still had women's hair in them. He habitually cut the hair curler from a random woman's hair while still in her hair and ran away.

Police had the original woman who was attacked down near the canal look at him to see if he was the one who attacked her. She claimed that she knew who he was and that they had been together before. So, the police had to let him go. But later, after some pressure from detectives, she changed her story and said that it was Danilov who attacked her. He was arrested and charged, and there was a lot of press that they had captured the attacker.

Meanwhile, in another part of town, the real killer struck again. This time, Filippenko sexually assaulted and murdered Valentina Stennikova, who was working at a fish market near the canal. After he killed her, he dumped her body in the river. Police found Stennikova's body, and after analyzing her, they realized that it was the same attacker who was responsible for her death, too.

Even though police were aware that the man they had in custody wasn't the killer, they would falsify the report so as not to cause a scandal. Detectives released to the press that the victim, Stennikova, had committed suicide and was not murdered. Her parents protested to the prosecutor's office without any success.

In early 1968, Filippenko traveled to Yalta for his job. While there, he attacked and tried to rape a maid. This time, he was caught. He was arrested and put in jail. While in his jail cell, he confessed to several of his previous murders in Leningrad to his cellmate, who happened to be a police informant.

The local police informed the capital police, who sent out some of their detectives to interrogate Filippenko. During this interview, Filippenko gave them detailed information about the five murders that happened around the Obvodny Canal. They transferred him to the Leningrad jail while they verified his confessions.

Police then dropped all charges against Danilov, and he was released. The six detectives who had arrested Danilov were fired from their jobs. The imprisoned Igor Vorobyev was also released.

Initially, Filippenko began to act like he was crazy or insane, so the court ordered him to be examined by a psychiatrist. But they found him fit to stand trial.

In the Fall of 1968, Filippenko was tried and convicted of five murders and five rapes and sentenced to death. In November 1968, he was executed by firing squad in Moscow.

EIGHT

Boris Korneev

THE STRONGMAN KILLER

Boris Korneev was a circus performer who was born in 1929 or 1930. Exactly where or when he was born has never been uncovered, and information about his parents or childhood is not known either. When he died in

1968, he claimed to be thirty-eight years old. The first time any documentation about Korneev appeared was when he placed ads in a Moscow newspaper.

Korneev was considered very strong because he constantly juggled weights and performed several strongman acts as a circus worker. He often showed off his strength by lifting weights in front of people and made a big deal about it.

In 1968, after Korneev finished a year-long run with a circus, he took his savings and moved to Voskresensk, Moscow Oblast. He figured he could take some time off and get a job later in the Summer for another circus. But he had run through most of his money after a few months. He was also unhappy that he wasn't famous or getting the attention that he figured he deserved where he was living.

Korneev decided to advertise for a roommate to help pay the bills. Yulia Trofimova answered his ad, and they liked each other a lot, so she moved in with him along with her eleven-year-old daughter, Oksana. The three started to live as a family.

Without Yulia knowing it, Korneev also placed an advertisement to meet other women for sex and possibly start a family. Two different women responded that Korneev liked, so he began to go out and meet them. He told Yulia that he was looking for a job so she wouldn't get suspicious. In truth, Korneev was having a separate life with three different women.

During this time, one of the women, Irina Schelkunova, became pregnant with Korneev's child. She demanded that he marry her and kept asking him every day. On one of these days, Korneev got angry, lost his temper, and strangled her to death by using a wire. She was twenty weeks pregnant at that time.

He then took her body into the industrial part of town, took her to the top of a building, and threw her off the roof into a parking lot. Her body landed on a bus that had been parked there. The bus driver was away from the bus in a café eating at the time her body landed on the bus. When he returned from lunch, he didn't notice the body on his bus's roof.

The bus driver exited the parking lot and started his bus route again. When he made his first stop to pick up passengers, the body fell onto the road. One of the men waiting at the bus stop ran over to the body to try and help her but soon realized that she was already dead.

Police were called and quickly saw the wire

marks on her neck and knew she had been strangled. It wasn't long before detectives were able to trace which building her body was thrown from and establish who she was.

When police interviewed Schelkunova's mother, they learned that she would often meet men from ads in the newspaper. One of the ads that she had responded to was from Sergi Poganovsky. When two detectives arrived at Poganovsky's house, his dog viciously attacked one of them, and the cops shot his dog. They arrested Poganovsky and took him in for questioning.

During their interrogation, Poganovsky admitted to placing ads in the paper and responding to ad females who advertised. Even though he was married, he would meet up with different women to have sex, and once he had sex with a woman, he dropped her. He could not supply a good alibi for the day that Schelkunova was murdered.

Shortly after this murder, Korneev was with Natalya Delyagina, and the two of them were drinking at her place when she told him that she had been abused by her stepmother, Galina, for years. After Natalya's father died, her stepmother would make her have sex with men as payment for them to do things around the house for her, like cutting wood for the fireplace.

Later that night, after the two parted, Korneev headed over to confront Galina, which escalated into a physical fight. His first murder seemed to bring something alive in Korneev's soul, and he enjoyed the murder. Korneev ended up strangling her to death and afterward took her body to the local quarry in the town and tied her to one of the vehicles that had been left there overnight.

After this murder, Korneev started to get rougher with Yulia and her daughter, Oksana. He began to chain Oksana to a fifty-kilogram weight, one he used when he worked for the circus, and have sex with her. Korneev would tell Yulia that constantly chaining Oksana would strengthen her for sports.

One day, Oksana's father came to visit her and found her chained up. He confronted Korneev, and the two left the house and went outside to fight. Korneev ended up killing Oksana's father by breaking his neck, and he took the body and dropped it off a cliff in a nearby park.

The following day, police found the body of Galina and noticed that she had been strangled the same way and with the same type of wires that Schelkunova had been. After questioning Galina's stepdaughter, Delyagina, they discovered that Galina had been abusing her. They wanted to know who else knew about this abuse and, specifically, if a boyfriend knew. She told them that she had told a guy she was seeing but refused to tell the police who this guy was. She said that she was thrilled and thankful that somebody had killed Galina.

Police decided to place surveillance on Delyagina's house to see who she was interacting with. The next evening, Korneev came over to her house and spotted the police officer watching her house. He snuck out and attacked the officer from behind and strangled him to death.

Korneev had already seen the press report about Galina's body being found and was worried about Delyagina telling police about him. So Korneev decided to murder her as well. He asked Delyagina if she would go to the park and have a lovely afternoon, and she agreed. Once they arrived, he steered them to a private place away from anyone else, strangled her, and then hid her body amongst some loose branches.

Early the following day, the body of the murdered officer was discovered when another officer came to Delyagina's house to relieve him.

The officer also couldn't find Delyagina, and an all-out search began for her that afternoon.

That same morning, Yulia decided to take her daughter Oksana to stay with her grandmother for a while, and when she returned to her house, Korneev was there waiting for her. He got furious at her when she told him she had taken Oksana to her grandmother's, and he started slapping her. Korneev then called Yulia's mother's house, and Oksana answered. He told her that she was to return home immediately or he would kill her mother.

Instead of calling the police or telling her grandmother, Oksana called her boyfriend, Misha, and told him what had happened. He told her that he would help her.

Later that evening, just after it turned dark, Misha and Oksana took a knife and hammer and went to Yulia's house. Instead of entering through the main door, Oksana walked down to the front of the garage, stood holding the knife behind her back, and waited. Misha hid behind a tree beside the driveway.

Korneev soon noticed Oksana standing outside in front of the garage, so he went out the front door and approached her smiling. When he was near enough, Oksana swung her arm around from behind her and stabbed the knife into his chest. The stab wound didn't seem to phase him at all, and he continued to walk right up to her and stood face to face within inches before grabbing her. She was in shock that Korneev didn't seem to be hurt.

Misha jumped out from behind the tree and hit Korneev over the head with the hammer. Korneev still didn't fall. He turned around, grabbed Misha, and threw him against the tree. He then turned back towards Oksana and started walking to her again. Just before he could grab hold of her, Korneev suddenly fell to the ground and passed out.

Soon, the police and an ambulance arrived, where they treated Misha and Oksana. Misha could not walk properly for a few years from hitting the tree so hard when he was thrown. Korneev was taken to the hospital, and they were able to save his life.

He was transferred to a mental hospital for evaluation before he could be tried for his crimes. The rumors of who he was and what he had done spread around town and the mental hospital like wildfire.

About one week later, Korneev was found

strangled to death in his hospital room, and nobody was ever arrested for his murder.

NINE

Vladimir Sulima

THE BLOODY CASANOVA

Vladimir Stepanovich Sulima was born in 1946. When and where Vladimir was born was never recorded, but we do know that he was born into a family that belonged to a religious sectarian cult. He was forced to read prayers and worship from as early as he could remember. His father was violent and often beat him with everything from metal pipes to a whip. Once, his father even placed him in a barrel and threw it down a large mountain, causing Vladimir to lose consciousness.

In 1960, by the age of fourteen, Vladimir was regularly having sex with both men and women. After getting into an argument with one of the men he was having sex with, Vladimir shot the man. After the shooting, Vladimir started attacking and raping women and men. By the time he was caught and arrested two years later when he was 16, he was charged with having committed thirteen rapes. He was sentenced to eight years as a minor but only served half that. By 1966, he was out, got a job, married, and had a child.

In March 1968, Vladimir committed his first murder. He attacked Galina Belonozhko and sexually assaulted her. When he was finished, he hit her over the head several times with a stick until she died. Vladimir attacked and raped nine other women after that, killing two more. Vladimir wasn't scared of his victims seeing him while he committed his assaults. Several witnesses were able to describe him to police.

One day, a victim of Vladimir's went to a clinic to see a doctor, and while she was in the waiting room, Vladimir walked in. She recognized him immediately. She was frightened, so she left to go home to call the police. By the time the police arrived at the clinic, he was gone. But he had forgotten his medical card with the check-in nurse there.

Police went to Vladimir's house and arrested him. He confessed to everything on his first interrogation. Later, he was convicted of three murders and sentenced to death. Vladimir was executed by firing squad on November 25, 1968.

TEN

Anatoly Utkin

THE ULYANOVSKY MANIAC

Anatoly Viktorovich Utkin was born in 1943 in Ulyanovsk while his father was away fighting in World War II. The exact date of his birth is not known. When his father, Viktor, returned from the war and discovered that his wife was pregnant, he accused her of having an affair and believed that the baby couldn't possibly be his. His father left the family. There were stories that Anatoly's mother attempted to abort him when she and his father were fighting about him belonging to another man. She was not successful.

Despite his father leaving the family, Anatoly appeared to have a somewhat normal childhood. His mother didn't tell him why she wasn't with his dad. He attended school regularly, and his first job was as a driver for the Soviet Union army.

Anatoly committed his first murder on March 31, 1968, when he was twenty-five. He spotted a fourteen-year-old girl walking in Barysh. He somehow managed to talk her into getting in his car. Her body wasn't found for two months, over three hundred kilometers from where she went missing. Anatoly kept the girl's watch.

On June 27th of that same year, Anatoly saw a seventeen-year-old walking home from school. Again, he somehow convinced her to get in his car. He raped and killed her. Three months later, in September, he did the same with a thirteen-year-old girl in Penza.

Anatoly attacked another girl on October 8th, but she was able to get away from him without any significant injuries. Unaffected, he attacked and murdered a ten-year-old the following month. He took the girl's sock from her left foot as a trophy. In May 1969, he murdered another girl in his hometown. Then he attempted to attack and rob another girl, but this time, he was caught and arrested for that one attack.

Anatoly was tried and sentenced to serve three years in prison. He was released from jail in October 1972 and, within a month, attacked another girl using the same method. The girl managed to break away and escape from him.

On December 6, 1972, Anatoly killed his only male victim that is known.

On February 8, 1973, Anatoly walked into a textile factory and tried to rob them. He killed the cashier and tried to open their safe to get their money, but it wouldn't open. Angry, he set the building on fire using a bucket of fuel and left.

The following day, police found the bucket Anatoly had accidentally left at the scene. It had his name engraved so nobody could steal it. He was arrested and charged with the crime. After all the evidence was collected, he was charged with nine murders, theft, and robbery. He was convicted on all charges and sentenced to death. Anatoly was executed by firing squad on September 12, 1975.

ELEVEN

Boris Serebryakov

THE NIGHT CREATURE

Boris Efimovich Serebryakov was born in Malgobek on August 18, 1941. From very early on in his childhood, Boris was a handful. He started to drink alcohol by the age of six and frequently got into fights with other boys around the neighborhood. As a young teen, he was often detained by police for causing problems.

Boris joined the military when he finished school in the Summer of 1959 and remained there until January 1967. After leaving the military, he moved in with his sister, who lived in Kuybyshev, and got a job at a cable-making plant.

On September 4, 1967, Boris tried to rape Yekaterina Kharitonova, a dispatcher at a tram depot. He only wore his bathing suit and ran into a control room where she worked. There, he grabbed her and, at knifepoint, tried to assault her sexually. She screamed and put up a fight. Boris began stabbing her, hitting her in her neck and both arms. She kept fighting and yelling, and Boris, getting nervous, ran away.

The next known attack by Boris happened almost two years later, in April 1969. He broke into a twenty-four-unit apartment building owned by a plant that housed their employees. Boris broke the window of the living room to one of the apartments and killed Stephan Zorkin, his wife, Maria, and their five-year-old son. He killed them all by hitting them over the head with a brick. After killing them, he raped the dead wife and ransacked their apartment, taking one hundred and thirty-five rubles. Afterward, he set the apartment on fire and left. Several other units were destroyed before the fire was put out. At first, police suspected Maria's ex-husband of the murders and fire.

A year passed by before Boris struck again. On April 30, 1970, he broke into another apartment building. This time, he took an axe with him. He found an apartment unit that had its front door unlocked. It belonged to the landlady, Ekaterina Kutsevalova, who lived with her five-year-old daughter. He hit them both over their heads with the back of the axe until they were unconscious. Boris began to assault Ekaterina sexually when the daughter Olga awakened and started to yell at the top of her lungs. Hearing her screams, the neighbors woke up, came out of their apartments, and entered the hallway. Boris got scared and ran away from the building. They both survived.

Boris decided that he would change where and how he found his victims. He got a bicycle and started riding it around town, searching for his victims. On the late night of May 7, 1970, during one of his bike rides, he murdered two people. Praskovya Salova, a seventy-year-old, and Nina Vasilieve, a thirty-year-old, both with his axe. During this time, another man went to the police and claimed that he had been the killer, but it wasn't long before the police figured out that he was a mentally ill man looking for attention.

A month later, on June 5, 1970, a family who lived in the Oktyabrsky District of town, a family of four Malomanovs, was found murdered. All of them were hacked to death with an axe. After they had been killed, the wife was raped before the house was set on fire.

It was voting time, and the murders had created such a panic most people stayed home and refused to go out unless they had to, even for voting. The police began patrols of the neighborhoods where they specifically looked at all cyclists.

On June 8, 1970, a member of the police patrol noticed Boris riding his bike on a street close to the airport. At first, he didn't think much of Boris until his jacket blew open from the wind. The officer noticed the axe under his coat. The officer yelled out and began to chase Boris, who fled and ran through a house's yard and into a street bathroom, where he hid.

While officers and some of the homeowners began to search the property, one of them opened the toilet door, and Boris hit them on the head with his axe. Boris ran and headed for the train station. He noticed a freight train starting to pull out there, so he jumped aboard. The engineer saw him get on the train and yelled at him, so Boris jumped off and ran away.

Boris arrived at the Progress Rocket Space lab and jumped their fences. Only that set their alarms off. It was their security team that captured him. He was turned over to police, who took his blood and fingerprints. They sent a unit to search his apartment as well.

His prints and blood type matched the murders. In his apartment, they found several items that had belonged to different victims. He initially claimed that he had a mental illness, but after an evaluation by the court psychiatrist was done, he was ruled fit to stand trial.

Boris was convicted of nine murders and sentenced to death. He was executed by firing squad early in 1971.

TWELVE

Yuri Raevsky

THE CHILD OF VICE

Yuri Nikolayevich Raevsky was born in Penza in 1952 to a wealthy family who worked for the Communist Party. At school, he was part of a special group for children of party members, where they were trained and educated to become party members when they became older. These children were taught party ethics and how to become leaders themselves.

In the Summer of 1968, just after Yuri turned sixteen years old, he was accused of a sexual assault on one of his female neighbors. After a psychological evaluation, he was found competent to stand trial. He was convicted and sent to a boy's correction school in Mordovian, about thirty kilometers from his home. This camp often made the boys do hard labor and sent them out to build things for the government.

During his time at this school, he was sexually assaulted by several of the older male inmates. It happened often enough that they tattooed a rose on his lower back, which, in prison, signified that he was an easy conquest for other male prisoners.

By the Summer of 1971, Yuri had escaped the boy's school. He went to Saransk, where he convinced an older woman to invite him into her house. Once inside, he beat, strangled, and raped her several times. Eventually, he left her for dead. However, she survived the attack but was forever handicapped from the injuries she received during the attack.

Next, Yuri moved to Moscow, where he began to rape and kill women regularly. He would go to train stations, parks, or other places to look for women who were tourists. Using his charm, he often gave them a rose and offered to take them around to show them the sights. As soon as he had them in a private location, he would attack them by hitting them over the head. As soon as they lost their balance, he would pull out a knife and stab them to death. He would then rape their corpse and leave the flower that he gave them on their bodies.

Yuri's first murder was in Moscow on August 30, 1971. When the victim's body was discovered near an airport and identified, police started questioning people who were at the airport when she was. They learned she was with a man, later identified as her boyfriend. He became the prime suspect, especially after they discovered the two had recently broken up.

While the boyfriend of the victim was in custody, Yuri killed again. Then, a third murder and rape was committed on September 14th. After that, panic surged through the city.

The public prosecutor took charge of the case, and during their investigation, they found no fingerprints or semen left at the crime scene. The second and third victims both carried their passports with them, but both had been destroyed, which made it more challenging to identify the victims.

With the third victim, a witness was found who mentioned to police that they had seen a man talking to the victim, who was wearing a smaller-fitting t-shirt, and they noticed a tattoo on the man's lower back. During a police check, they discovered Yuri had escaped prison and had a tattoo on his lower back. After showing the witness pictures of Yuri, he was positively identified and became a suspect in all three crimes.

About ten days after the last murder, Yuri met a girl in the park area of town. As they were walking through a park, they passed a police officer. The police officer noticed the woman was carrying a rose. Knowing that each of the victims in the recent wave of killings had been found with a rose left on their bodies, he stopped and turned to approach the couple to make sure everything was okay. Yuri bolted and escaped. He decided to leave Moscow after the close call.

Yuri then moved to Klaipeda and attacked again after only two weeks. This time, he was hanging around a tourist site called Klaipeda Castle, where a group of archaeologists were working. He was able to lure one of the tourists away from her group and talk her into going for a walk. Once they were hidden from the rest of the group, Yuri sexually assaulted her and murdered her with a knife, stabbing her fourteen times.

While fleeing the crime scene, Yuri dropped his passport on the ground. Some school-aged children near the site saw Yuri drop his passport, so they picked it up and chased him to give it back. When Yuri saw the kids chasing and yelling at him, he worried they might have seen something. So he kept moving away from them as he didn't want them to catch him. To get out of the Castle property, you had to be let out through a check center, so while Yuri was stopped there, the kids caught up with him and gave him back his passport. Yuri left, but his strange behavior made the kids suspicious. So they told the guards at the checkpoint about what happened. They knew his name as they had just read it while reviewing the passport.

Yuri continued moving from town to town. His first stop after leaving Klaipeda Castle was Mineralnye Vody. He only remained there for a couple of days after he raped and murdered another woman. Even though that murder was not connected to all of the other murders, Yuri fled that town just to be safe. Later, during his arrest and trial, police would become aware that Yuri was the attacker in this case as well.

Yuri next headed for the city of Kharkiv, which was the second largest city in the Ukraine. At the end of October, he sexually assaulted and murdered a local woman. The following day, Yuri began to sell off his victim's possessions. When he tried to sell her coat, he was arrested.

During his arrest, the police were very cordial with him. They didn't know then that he was the mad murderer on the loose throughout the region. They thought he was just a thief. He was taken to jail and booked for theft. The warden on duty had written a pass for Yuri to leave with his promise to appear in court on the theft charges later.

Yuri was mere minutes away from being released when the police received confirmation that the coat Yuri was trying to sell belonged to the victim of a murder they were investigating. He remained in jail until a complete investigation was completed.

Yuri was ultimately charged and tried for six murders in 1972. He was found guilty and sentenced to death. On December 8, 1973, Yuri was executed by firing squad in Moscow.

THIRTEEN

Gennady Ivanov

THE BEAST

Gennady Ivanovich Ivanov was born in Chuvash, ASSR, in 1947. Not much is known about his family or childhood. As a young adult, Gennady served in the Baikonur secret military police until it was disbanded in early 1973. During that time, Gennady got into an argument with his girlfriend, which turned physical. She died from her injuries. He was arrested and charged with manslaughter. Gennady was quickly convicted and sentenced to ten years in prison. After only seven years in jail, he was granted parole.

Once out of prison in 1980, he got a job with a car manufacturer, Gorkovsky. This job would only last a few months as he preferred not to work and found it easier to rob people of their money. His first known offense after this was when he tried to sexually assault Anna Kovaleva, but during the attack, a couple who were out walking after dinner saw what was happening, and he fled.

Later that same night, Gennady attacked another woman and stabbed her several times before sexually assaulting her. She survived the attack and gave police a complete description of her assailant.

About two weeks later, Gennady attacked Nina Sinitsyna, sexually assaulting her and robbing her of two hundred rubles before stabbing her to death. He took the money he stole from her and bought some new clothes. His old clothing was all bloody from his assaults on people.

Two days after that, Gennady started following a man because he liked the shoes he was wearing. As soon as the man was walking in an area where nobody was around, Gennady attacked and killed the man for his boots. He left his old bloody shoes with the man's corpse in an alley.

Later that same afternoon, Gennady saw another man wearing shoes he liked. He followed that man, too, and did the same thing as he did with his previous male victim. Only this man carried about eleven hundred rubles, so he stole that and his shoes.

Two weeks later, he passed two women on a payphone: one was talking to someone while the other stood and waited. As he passed, he thought the two women had said something about him and laughed. Gennady turned around, came back to the payphone, and began stabbing both of them. Both died from their injuries, but one of them lived long enough to give the police his description.

The following week, Gennady robbed and killed a World War II veteran. The attack caused a great shock in the community. Later that same day, he got into an argument with a woman, killed her on the street, and fled the scene. Not even an hour after that, he attacked and sexually assaulted another woman, only this time he was caught and arrested.

Police searched Gennady's home and found items that belonged to several of his victims, including jewelry, watches, and clothing. As the police questioned him, he would only answer them if they addressed him as "The King."

Gennady was charged and convicted of eight murders and sentenced to death. He was executed in September 1982 by a firing squad in Moscow.

FOURTEEN

Valery Logvinov

THE HAIR HUNTER

Valery Zakharovich Logvinov was born sometime in the year 1950 in Saratov. He grew up in a poor household where his father, who had anger issues, often beat his mother in front of him. One thing that Valery specifically remembered was that his father used to grab his mother by her braid before hitting her because it gave him a good grip on her head. That image of his mother's braided hair stayed with him throughout his life.

After Valery graduated from school, he got a job as a tiler at a local factory. He was doing well enough within ten years to get his own house. Valery married after that and had a son in 1972. His wife often complained that he frequently went out at night after dinner, leaving her alone with their child while he went to bars and flirted with other women.

After a night of drinking, he usually went to the Zavodskiy District, where the government businesses were located. That area was vacant at night. Valery would wander the streets looking for lone females walking. He would approach her, initiate a conversation, and offer to walk her to where she was heading. Once they were isolated, he would pull out a small iron rod he was carrying and knock her out. After beating the woman into unconsciousness, he would sexually assault her. Once he was finished, he would discard their body in a garbage can or down a deserted alley.

Valery's first victim was thought to be in December 1974. Valentina Tuchkova, a ninety-two-year-old woman living in a nursing home with dementia, left the home to meet a friend of hers and never returned. She was later found walking around the streets with a bloody head. A passerby ran into her and took her to the hospital. When police arrived to question her about what had happened, she was confused and unable to tell them anything. Police initially thought that maybe she had just fallen and hit her head, so there was no concern.

On December 15th, Natalia Selyatina, a thirty-year-old, was walking home from work when suddenly Valery came out of an alley and hit her on the head, knocking her to the ground. He dragged her back into the alley where he came from and sexually assaulted her. Then, he fled. She was found and brought to the hospital but died before police could question her.

Just two days later, Valery attacked Tatyna Larina, a twenty-seven-year-old, in the same way by sneaking out of an alley and striking her on the head, dragging her back into the alley, sexually assaulting her, then leaving her when he was finished. Larina was found dead.

Only two days later, Valery repeated his killing spree with thirty-year-old Olga Igshina. Only this time, he was interrupted during the attack by another woman, Svetlana Bukhanova, a twenty-five-year-old, who scared him away. Igshina survived the attack, but because she was struck on her head, she was unable to remember anything about the attack.

Also in December, Valery attacked, raped, and killed forty-seven-year-old Raisa Dubova. He was almost caught again during the attack, and this led him to change his method of attacking women.

The following day, Valery went to an apartment building where the caretaker had left his ladder on the lawn. He used the ladder to break into a second-floor apartment where a couple slept. He attacked them both, knocking them out and then sexually assaulting the woman. She later died from her injuries. He also ransacked their apartment, taking several items with him.

After so many attacks, sexual assaults, and murders in such a short time, police started a special task force to catch the murderer. Realizing that the victims all had braided hair in common, they brought in a couple of policewomen who fit the general description of several victims and braided hair to act as bait. But noticing all the police around town, Valery stopped attacking women for a while.

Valery's next attack didn't happen until the Summer of 1975. He also changed the district of his murders to the Krasnokutsky district, which was also a business and government-style part of town. This time, he approached a fifty-year-old woman, Lyudmila Pavlikova, who was waiting at the rail station. He struck up a conversation with her and, when she wasn't looking, hit her over her head with the pipe and then sexually assaulted her. She survived.

The person who found her after the attack sought out a rail station worker, and they called the police. Once the police arrived, they roped off a large area surrounding the station and questioned the victim. The victim was able to give a description. Twelve men who were in the area when the attack happened were detained, brought to the police station, and questioned. One of those men told the detectives that he was there with an acquaintance, Valery Logvinov, but that they didn't know where he went. Police searched for Valery at his home and detained him for questioning.

During questioning, Valery denied doing anything wrong. But once he was in a lineup, survivor Svetlana Bukhanova picked him out instantly. When she pointed to Valery in the lineup, her finger touched his chest, and he responded by asking her to touch him sexually.

After the lineup, he confessed to police about all of his attacks.

Valery was charged with seven murders and seven rapes, and in 1976 was convicted of the seven murders but only six of the rapes. He was sentenced to death. He initially filed an appeal to the death sentence, but it was rejected. He was executed by firing squad in 1977.

FIFTEEN

Vladimir Usov

BOY HUNTER

Vladimir Aleksandrovich Usov was born to a working-class family in Kazan, Soviet Union, sometime in 1957. As with so many others, there are no records of the exact date or place of birth. Both of his parents drank a lot and often called Vladimir names and made fun of him.

When Vladimir turned eleven, he began hearing voices in his head that told him what to do. One voice told him he shouldn't be going to school. So, he started skipping classes and instead went to the local park and hung around until it was time for him to be home from school. His parents scolded him once they heard Vladimir wasn't attending classes. He told them that he was quitting school.

His parents decided to take Vladimir to a psychiatrist to try and figure out what was wrong with him, and maybe they could convince him to go back to school. The doctor diagnosed Vladimir as a paranoid schizophrenic. He was placed on medication and forced to return to fifth grade.

Not long after returning, Vladimir told all his classmates and teachers that he was conversing with an invisible being from outer space. This being would ask him to do weird things, such as making himself a jam sandwich even when he wasn't hungry. Vladimir believed the voice was preparing him for a top-secret mission. After hearing these stories, his parents took him back to his psychiatrist, who decided that he needed to be on more extreme medications and that he should not return to school. Later, once he reached 14, his condition allowed him to receive a disability pension from the government.

Over the next three years, Vladimir stayed home, drank alcohol, and did nothing. He claimed the voices were getting worse and demanded more of him, but his parents and doctor did nothing about it. The voices became more sinister, and they began to demand that Vladimir have sex with young boys, which at first scared him. By the Summer of 1974, at the age of 17, he began doing what the voices told him to do.

On July 30th, eight-year-old Boris M. never returned from playing with his friends. The next day, his family began to search for him and learned from one of his friends, Alexei V., that Boris had been playing with a man in a blue suit who approached the boys and asked if they wanted to collect nuts from their local park. Boris was the only one who went with the man. He never returned.

Police were called, and they began their investigation of the missing boy. Boris' body was found just two kilometers from the park where he went with the man. The medical examiner's report said that Boris had been strangled to death and he was violently sexually assaulted. They couldn't find much evidence around the body as it had been raining hard during the days following his disappearance.

One week later, on August 8th, Vladimir found himself in Upravlenchesky, about one hundred kilometers from where he lived. He ran into Oleg L. and offered the boy some candy. They walked and talked on their way to their local park. Once there, Vladimir sexually assaulted Oleg, who began to cry loudly during the attack. Vladimir hit him over the head, knocking him out. After he was finished, he stabbed the boy to death. He was about to cut the boy's penis off so that he could take it home as a souvenir when he heard a group of people coming towards him. Oleg's body wasn't discovered for two weeks.

While Vladimir was returning home, his bus stopped at the Togliatti station. Seven-year-old Valeria R. was waiting for the bus with his mother and her friend. Just as the bus pulled into the station, Valeria asked his mother if he could go to the bathroom. She was getting their luggage on the bus, so she told him to hurry up and go. After about fifteen minutes, when the boy didn't return, his mother and her friend went looking for him. Once they realized the boy wasn't in the bathroom, she told the bus station employees, who called the police. After the police arrived, they started to search for Valeria. They would find his dead body lying face down in a field not far from the station. His pants had been pulled down to his knees, and he had apparent bruises on his head.

After the murder of Valeria, detectives focused their attention on a teacher, Petr Popov, because some of their informants had told them that he was a homosexual. They took Popov in for questioning, and he admitted to being a homosexual and having had sexual relations with other men. Under duress, he also confessed to the rape and murder of two of the victims. As a result, he was fired from his job as a teacher, and he even tried to hang himself while in jail.

Eventually, detectives would realize that Popov was not the man who had been attacking these young boys. The only person he wanted to kill was himself, but he wasn't brave enough to do it. He wanted the country to do it for him. His life had been ruined for being exposed as a homosexual.

Meanwhile, Vladimir continued his attack on young boys. On April 10, 1975, he began riding his bicycle around town looking for a victim. He saw seven-year-old Andrei M. playing on the front lawn of a boarding house. He stopped and talked the boy into going into the back garden of the house. When he started to take the boy's pants off, the boy screamed. Vladimir grabbed the boy by his neck and began to choke him until he went unconscious. He heard two men walking on the path behind the house, so he grabbed the boy's body and stuffed it into a concrete chimney that was lying in the garden. Then, he left on his bike. The two men noticed the boy's feet sticking out of the chimney, so they pulled him out. Andrei regained consciousness and told them what had happened. Soon, the whole neighborhood was out looking for the attacker, but he was already gone.

Two months later, on June 17, 1975, when Vladimir was out riding his bike again looking for a victim, he ran into two boys, eleven-year-old Sasha Y. and Tolya S. He told the boys that he had some fresh strawberries at his home in the garden and said that they were welcome to come over and eat some. He placed both kids on his bike and began to take them home. Halfway there, he stopped the bike and told Tolya to get off because he couldn't handle riding with both of them on the bike. Once off the bike, Vladimir took off again with just Sasha.

Vladimir ended up taking Sasha to a park, where he strangled him until he passed out and then sexually assaulted him. Once he was finished, he stabbed the boy in the chest and stomach. This time, Vladimir decided to dispose of the body, so he put the body on some wood and set it on fire. As the fire raged and the smell of burning flesh got into Vladimir's face, he dropped his bike and walked home without it.

Later, when police arrived to find the body, they also found Vladimir's bike. The bike was the item that not only led police to Vladimir but also became a large piece of evidence used in the trial after detectives found fingerprints and other traces of evidence from the bike.

Police arrested Vladimir by the end of that Summer, and during his first interrogation, he confessed to having murdered Sasha and then told them about two other boys he had done the same thing to earlier that same year. He was able to describe in great detail what he had done to each of the boys he had assaulted.

During their investigation, police had several witnesses come forward who could identify Vladimir. The Moscow Serbsky Institute also examined Vladimir and confirmed the diagnosis of him being a paranoid schizophrenic. The court decided that due to his mental illness, he could not be held criminally liable and was sent for mandatory treatment at a psychiatric hospital.

SIXTEEN

Andrei Evseev

THE TAGANSKY MANIAC

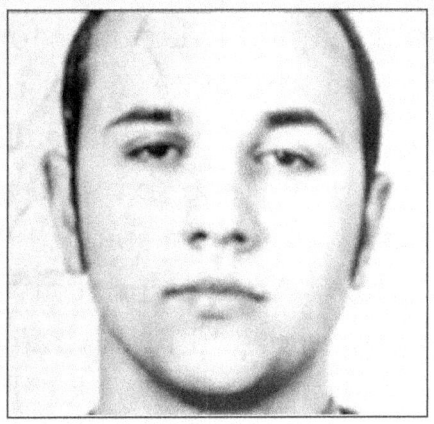

Andrei Nikoalevich Evseev was born in 1955 in Kholkovo, Soviet Union. His parents were not very strict and allowed him to do whatever he wanted. He often skipped school and hung out with his friends, and he quit school during the seventh grade. After that, he did odd jobs around town.

By the early 1970s, when he was just sixteen years old, Andrei was placed in a psychiatric hospital for evaluation because he often felt uncontrollable anger. He was given medications to try and calm him down. Later, he would claim that the hospital injected him with several drugs, which caused him more pain. He began to hate all the employees there.

Andrei was released from the clinic in the early part of 1974. On August 24th, he met a sixteen-year-old named Marina Morozova, who he noticed because she wore an all-red outfit. He lured her into an isolated area and killed her.

The next day, he met sixty-six-year-old chef Gennady Kuzman at a train station. After the two talked for a while, Andrei suddenly stabbed the man to death, robbed him, and dragged his body into a ditch beside the train tracks. The chef had a food order receipt for a chicken and some peaches in his pocket. Later, when Andrei attempted to pick up the order, he was arrested.

During the interrogation by police, he admitted to murdering the sixteen-year-old schoolgirl the day before but not the chef. Police were not interested in what he was telling them about the Morozova murder, or they didn't believe him. Instead, they were trying to prove he was involved with the chef's murder. Unable to come up with anything, they released him.

Andrei decided to move to Moscow the following month. Once there, he began another rampage, starting with attacking a student, Vladimir Parshin, who had been walking through the park on his way home. Andrei stabbed him several times with a knife and robbed him. Vladimir survived the attack.

The following day, on September 24th, he broke into a house near the Dobryninskaya Train Station. There, he attacked and robbed the resident Anna Astafyeva. After he fled the house, she called for help and was taken to the hospital. She was able to describe her attacker to police before she died from her injuries the following day.

Two days after that, Andrei was at the forty-third train station in Moscow and ran across a man who looked very similar to himself. He decided that he would first kill this man, then change clothes with him so it would hopefully fool the police into thinking that the dead man was the attacker they were looking for. He snuck up on the man from behind and stabbed him in the back.

But when Andrei tried to pull the knife out, it broke in half.

He took the handle of the knife and fled the scene. The man was found still alive and taken to the hospital, where he later died. Police discovered the victim was Nikolai Dyomin, a convicted thief and murderer who had just recently been released from a twenty-year prison sentence. Andrei's plan worked, and the detectives assumed that Dyomin was the man who had committed the previous murders.

On October 8, 1974, Andrei attacked and robbed three different women in the Tagansky district of Moscow, all of whom were wearing red outfits. He stabbed each of them and took their purses. Two of these victims died from their knife wounds. When the city of Moscow heard about the attacks, everyone began to panic, and the media called the attacker the "Killer of Women in Red."

One week later, on October 15th, Andrei committed another robbery spree. This time, he was hanging around the Akademicheskaya Metro Station, looking for his victims. Within the short span of twenty minutes, he assaulted two more women who were wearing red dresses in the same way, stabbing them and stealing their purses. One of the victims died from her knife wounds.

The following day, Andrei did it again. But this time, it was at the Proletarskaya Metro Station, and neither victim was wearing red. Again, he stabbed the woman, took their purse, and again, one of the two victims died from their knife wound.

After this series of attacks, Nikolai Schelokov, the Minister of Internal Affairs for the USSR, went on television and told people to be extremely careful and for women not to go out alone. He also said a special police task force was created to deal with the attacker. The warning scared Andrei into stopping his attacks for about two years until the panic in the city dwindled.

In early November 1977, Andrei began his robberies again, attacking four different women within the month. Two of the victims died from their wounds, but this time, instead of a knife, he used a screwdriver. He also changed his MO further because, in the case of one of the women that he attacked, robbed, and murdered, he also raped her after she was dead. She was the wife of a famous Soviet artist, Mikhail Kupriyanov.

Even with all the news media reports about Andrei's latest murders, he went on to attack again only a month later, on December 19th. This time, he attacked and killed Lydia Schur, where several witnesses could see him in front of a popular housewares store located in Sofrino. He stole not only her money but her watch, jewelry, and a dog collar.

After police took all of the witness statements from those who saw the attack from the store, they arrested Andrei on December 28th. At first, he refused to cooperate with the detectives during their interviews. When his apartment was searched, the only thing detectives found was a dog collar, but none of the other jewelry that had been stolen from the victims. Astonishingly, Andrei had used the jewels that he took from his victims to decorate his Christmas tree. They never spotted any of it there.

When they asked him about the dog collar, Andrei claimed that it was a collar from his dog, who had died years before, and that he had kept it as a memory of his dog. While Andrei was in jail, he told one of his cellmates, a police informant, that his mother had probably already baked some pies with the jewelry.

Police searched Andrei's apartment again and found the stolen jewels in a flour bag in the kitchen. He eventually confessed to nine murders, eighteen attempted murders, one rape, and thirty-two robberies.

Andrei was examined and found competent to stand trial, where he was convicted on all charges and sentenced to death. In early 1979, he was executed by firing squad.

SEVENTEEN

Nikolai Shestakov

THE LUBERETSKY MANIAC

Nikolai Porfirievich Shestakov was born sometime in 1954 and lived in the metropolitan area of Moscow. Nothing is known about his family or upbringing. He only became known to the police or the public after he was arrested on March 12, 1976, for murdering twelve women and attempting to murder four others. He had two accomplices.

Shestakov, a truck driver, along with his friend, Andrei Vladimirovich Shuvalov, and younger sixteen-year-old brother Vladimir Shestakov, usually picked up girls waiting at a bus stop. The older Shestakov would hit them over the head with a sledgehammer that he carried in his truck. After they were unconscious or dead, he would rape them, take anything of value that they had on them, and then dump their remains in garbage dumps.

After the arrest, police found the sledgehammer used to murder the girls, which still had blood on it. The blood matched some of the victims. In his apartment and truck, they also found several items, including clothing, that they could match to his victims.

During the trial in 1977, Nikolai was convicted of all charges and sentenced to death. His friend Shuvalov was sentenced to fifteen years as an accomplice, and his young brother was sentenced to only four years as he was still a minor. Nikolai was executed by firing squad.

EIGHTEEN

Vladimir Sarenpya

THE ALEXANDROVSKY RIPPER

V ladimir Ronaldovich Sarenpya was born in Coos Bay, Oregon, United States, to a Finnish couple in 1949. The family was communist and decided they wanted to raise their family in the USSR, so they moved there as soon as his mother had recovered from giving birth to Vladimir.

As a young adult, Vladimir worked as a bus driver for Aleksandrovsky Motor Transport Enterprises. He soon married and moved into his own place, where they had two daughters. It was around this time that he made his first attack on a woman.

On September 27, 1975, Vladimir pulled over to the roadside after passing a woman on a bike, Nadezhda B., in Baksheevo. As she approached him, she slowed down to ask him if he needed help. Vladimir lunged at her, making her lose balance and fall off her bike. He jumped on her and began hitting her in the head. She broke away from him, got up, and ran towards town.

Vladimir grabbed a rock and began to chase her down the road. Once he caught up with her, he started hitting her with it. After she fell to the ground again, Vladimir told her if she stopped screaming, he would stop hitting her. They both stood up, and he led her back towards his truck.

She broke away again and started running and yelling again. Vladimir began to chase her again, but this time, a motorcyclist started driving towards them from the other direction. About to get caught, Vladimir dropped the rock, ran back to his truck, and fled. The biker stopped and took Nadezhda to the hospital.

Vladimir had a dream to become famous by being talked about for killing and raping women. He wanted there to be a city or even country-wide fear of him. Even though his first attempt didn't go as planned, within two months, on November 5th, he tried again.

While driving the Dvorikovsky highway, he noticed a woman, Nina A., walking alone. He pulled his truck over, got out, and started to hit her in the head with a wrench until she passed out. Before he had a chance to rape or kill her, a group of school kids who were walking the same road came towards them and began to scream at what they saw. So, again, Vladimir got into his truck and left.

Just over a week later, on November 14th, he noticed an eighteen-year-old, Tatyana A., waiting at the Aleksandrov Train Station to work as an equipment installer at the Aleksandrov Radio Plant. This time, he used a hammer to hit his victim, and this time, he hit Tatyana enough times to kill her. After he sexually assaulted her, he took her body and dumped it in the forest located close to the train station. To leave something that police would consider a calling card for each of his victims, Vladimir bit the neck of each of his victims—hard enough to draw blood and leave a mark.

Later that same day, Tatyana's body was discovered, and police were called. When her body was found, she was stripped naked, and all of her clothing and personal items were scattered around the area. Everything was covered with her blood. Police discovered a bloody hammer and a glove that belonged to a man, also covered with blood nearby. There were drag marks on her body from the train station to where she was found, making it easy for her to be discovered.

Detectives were also able to track Tayana's moves on her last day alive before the attack by questioning her friends, family, coworkers, and the railway employees who were on duty that day. Quite a few witnesses had noticed her walking but didn't see anyone following or talking to her. The case went cold.

Vladimir struck again after the holidays on January 16, 1976. Evgenia B., a thirty-year-old plant worker, returned home late after her shift. The streets were deserted as usual when she was walking home from work. Since it was late, she was used to it and wasn't apprehensive. She did pass a man during her walk home, but she never thought about it, as it was common for her to pass other workers walking home.

Just after he passed her, he turned around and began to hit her on the back of her head with a metal pipe. She fell to the ground but was still conscious. She fought back and managed to avoid being hit on the head again. After she started to scream, Vladimir got spooked for some reason, stopped hitting her, and ran away.

The police investigation stepped up their search again, but it was not soon enough to stop another attack. On March 6th, Nina P., a twenty-two-year-old, was found dead in a city park. She was dumped in a pile of coal, gagged with a noose made of her bra wrapped around her neck. Like previous victims, she had also been bitten on her neck and breasts hard enough to draw blood.

Police interviewed all of Nina's friends, family, and coworkers at the telephone station where she worked as an operator. One of the other employees told police that a man named Vladimir Sarenpya was waiting for Nina to get off work to walk her home. Nina had complained to her coworkers about Vladimir bugging her for weeks to go out with him, but she didn't want to date a married man.

Police brought Vladimir in for questioning about his involvement with Nina P. He claimed that he was sick that day, and instead of meeting Nina to walk her home from work, he was with a friend eating somewhere and didn't get home until eleven that night. But when the police checked with that friend, they found a different timeline. The friend said he dropped Vladimir off at his place that night.

After more interrogation, Vladimir admitted to having committed two murders and nine attempted murders and was charged.

Later, in 1976, the court found Vladimir guilty on all charges and sentenced him to death. He was later executed by one shot to the back of his head.

NINETEEN

Sergey Kashintsev

THE CANE KILLER

S ergey Alexandrovich Kashintsev was born on August 9, 1940, in Podyuga, Arkhangelsk, Soviet Union. His right leg was shorter than his left, which caused him to walk with a cane. As expected, several other kids teased and laughed at him when he started school. By the time he reached thirteen years old, he was having angry and loud outbursts at school and home. Sergey often yelled at his mother when she asked him to do homework.

At age fifteen, Sergey ran away from home and was soon arrested after he talked a girl into going into the bathhouse, where he sexually assaulted her. Sergey was never arrested or charged with that crime.

Early in 1970, Sergey was arrested for stealing his brother's coat from their apartment. When Sergey was released from jail, he refused to speak to his brother again, so instead of moving back in with him, he decided to move in with a friend. At first, he worked odd jobs to support himself. But often, these wouldn't last longer than a month or two.

Sergey started to threaten his landlady with a beating if she didn't give him some money. She started paying him a small amount every week, and when he asked for more, and she refused, he beat her each time until she gave him money. The landlady never called the police because she was too scared of him, but Sergey was arrested anyway for causing property damage and exposing himself to another woman. He spent two years in jail for this.

Once he got out of jail, he began to live on the street, where he would look for female drinking buddies to hang around with. Sergey would often end up getting into a fight with them and killing them, sometimes raping them in the process. Still, because they were homeless and usually unknown, police never spent much time trying to find the murderer of these women.

In 1975, Sergey finally got caught for murdering a homeless woman, Korotova T., and was arrested and charged with her murder. The court gave him a psychiatric examination and found him fit to stand trial. During the trial, it was proven that Sergey was drunk, so instead of receiving a life sentence, he was sentenced to ten years of hard labor in prison.

Sergey served his full ten-year sentence because he wasn't an exemplary prisoner. He often fought with the staff and other inmates, and he frequently called the female nurses who treated inmates sexually explicit names. He also refused to work or cooperate with the guards in any way, which led him to be put in solitary for most of his prison time. While in solitary confinement, Sergey read books on human anatomy, forensics, and trials.

Sergey knew he was no longer wanted by his family or the people in his hometown, so when he was released in 1985, he decided to travel around the country. He usually traveled on the trains in a car with other people who were homeless like he was. His MO was to strike up a conversation with a transient woman and convince her to go with him to a private area or empty car so that they could have sex. After they had sex, he would strangle and kill her. If the woman refused to go with him, he would wait for an opportunity to catch her alone, and he would beat her and sexually assault her before killing her.

The first murder that police were able to prove that Sergey committed was on January 8, 1986. He met fifty-seven-year-old Fyodorova, who was traveling to her home from work. They began talking at the railway station, and she invited him to her apartment. She wasn't living alone, so they drank and talked until everyone went to bed. In the middle of the night, Sergey grabbed he when she was asleep and dragged her into the bathroom, where he slammed her head against the bathtub, knocking her out. He then strangled her to death before leaving.

Over the following two years, Sergey continued to attack and kill several other women until April 28, 1957, when a couple of railroad employees saw him standing over a woman who was lying on the ground near the tracks. Shortly after, they saw Sergey leave, so they went over to check on the woman and found her dead. They called the police, who came out, and when searching the area, they found Sergey asleep in a place not too far away from the dead girl.

Once arrested and during interrogation, Sergey tried to pretend that he was insane. He even admitted to committing several murders that he couldn't possibly have done. After a thorough investigation, police charged him with eight murders, three attempted murders, and two counts of theft.

The court examined him and found that Sergey did have some organic brain damage and diagnosed him as having a psychopathic syndrome. But even with these issues, he was forced to stand trial.

After a two-month trial on March 13, 1990, Sergey was convicted of all charges and sentenced to death. On January 17, 1992, after a failed appeal attempt, he was executed by a single shot to the back of his head.

TWENTY

Fyodor Kozlov

THE MONSTER OF LOZHOK

Fyodor Nikolayevich Kozlov was born in Semiyarsk, Semipalatinsk, Kazakhstan, on April 9, 1959, but grew up in Rostov after his parents moved there shortly after his birth for work. Fyodor was a timid boy and socially awkward, making it hard for him to make friends. He spent all his time alone. The older he got, the worse he became. He began to skip school regularly, which caused several fights between him and his parents.

When Fyodor turned seventeen, his parents decided it would be best if he lived with his grandmother. She was the only person he seemed to like and get along with. On a Saturday afternoon in early 1976, Fyodor's eleven-year-old cousin was over for a visit. He talked her into coming into his room, where he proceeded to sexually assault her. When she screamed, his grandmother burst into the room to try and stop him. Fyodor ran out and grabbed an axe from the back of the house, came back to his bedroom, and hacked both of them to death.

Neighbors who heard the screaming and got no answer when they tried calling ended up calling the police. Fyodor was arrested and charged with two murders. His trial began in November 1976, and the court convicted him on both murder charges. Because he was seventeen years old, he was only sentenced to ten years in prison.

Fyodor served the whole ten years because he was not a cooperative prisoner. He constantly ignored the guards, didn't do what he was told, and often got into fights with other inmates. During his time there, he met and continued a relationship with a woman by mail. Once he completed his sentence and was released, he moved to Novosibirsk to be with her. The two of them got married that same year, in 1986.

Fyodor got a job as a welder so they could move into their own place. Shortly after that, they had a child. About six months after their child was born, his wife left him, taking their child and moving back in with her parents.

In June 1989, when Fyodor was living alone, he was taking the bus home from work when he saw a girl walking alone on an unpaved side road. She was an eighteen-year-old salesgirl named Natalya Rodnikova, who was heading home after she finished work. He got off the bus at the net stop and quickly caught up with her.

Fyodor pulled out a knife and made her walk into the bush, where he sexually assaulted her and stabbed her to death. He left her body there and returned home. Later that night, after thinking that her body might be found, he decided to go back to the crime scene, piled some branches over her body, and lit it on fire.

The following day, when Natalya's family was looking for her, her father came across a burnt corpse in the woods. He recognized the unburned shoes and dress on the body. Once police were notified about the murder, they thought about Fyodor as a possible suspect since he didn't live far away. Still, after talking to his boss and neighbors, they believed he was now living a law-abiding life.

The following month, in July, Fyodor was sent out to do a welding job at a factory in Iskitim. One day, after he finished his work, he was walking down a street when a twelve-year-old girl, Masha Dorofeeva, accidentally ran into him while riding her bike. He told the girl that he was a policeman and even showed her his strike workers permit—in the Soviet Union, trusted good employees would receive one from the government. He coerced the girl into walking to an abandoned two-story building. Once inside the house, he tied her up, gagged her, and then sexually assaulted her. When he was finished, he stabbed her in the neck and, after, lit her body on fire.

Only two days later, while Fyodor was still working in Iskitim, he approached a nineteen-year-old girl sitting alone at the beach. He sat beside her and asked her if she had a cigarette he could have. She reached for her purse to find him one, and he grabbed her and tried to tie her hands up. The girl was limber enough to escape his clutches and ran screaming. People nearby stood up and approached her. Fyodor got up and quickly fled the scene. After police were called, she gave them a pretty good description, so they made a wanted poster and posted it around the town.

With so much attention about an attacker in the town of Iskitim, he decided to go to a different city to continue his assaults. In the early part of

August, while he was walking around the streets of downtown Novosibirsk, he bumped into an eighteen-year-old girl, lured her to the bushes, attacked, raped, and killed her. He covered her body with branches and lit it on fire.

Two days later, he did the same thing again in the same town to a twenty-four-year-old woman. Both bodies were found, and the police started to send extra patrols out at night, as well as give several interviews to the media.

Later that month, Fyodor took a leave of absence from his job and visited his estranged wife and child at her parent's place in Omsk. While visiting Omsk, he walked alone one day and met an eleven-year-old girl on her front lawn playing alone. He managed to get her into the bushes, where he tied her hands and gagged her mouth. He then sexually assaulted her and stabbed her to death. Like his previous victims, he piled branches on her body and burned it.

When police found the burned corpse in the woods, they recognized the same thing had happened in some of the other nearby cities, so they contacted their police forces and created a joint task force to try and catch the murderer.

In September, Fyodor returned to Novosibirsk to his job. The very first night that he was there, he decided to attack a woman who was waiting at the train station. When he grabbed her hands to tie them, she fought back. She seemed much stronger than he thought she was. She also began yelling, attracting the attention of two firefighters in the rail station. He fled and managed to get away from them, but they were able to give a good description of the attacker to the police.

A few days later, the police had the victim and two witnesses come to the station to look through the mugshots. All three of them were able to identify Fyodor positively. Later that day, after issuing a warrant for his arrest, police spotted him at the bus stop, detained him, and brought him in for questioning.

During his interrogation, Fyodor confessed to five murders and five attempted murders, and by April 1990, he was placed on trial for seven murders and five attempted murders. He was found guilty on all charges and sentenced to death. He was sent to death row in Novosibirsk to be executed. On September 1, 1990, two days before his scheduled execution, he was found hanging in his cell.

TWENTY-ONE

Anatoly Biryukov

THE BABY HUNTER

Anatoly Nikolaevich Biryukov was born in the Lopasnya part of Moscow, which today is called Chekov, Moscow, on February 18, 1939. From all reports, Anatoly grew up in a relatively average middle-class home with no issues. After he finished school, he joined the military, becoming a general in the Soviet Army.

Suddenly, at age 38, Anatoly was walking in downtown Moscow on September 16, 1977, when he noticed a baby stroller parked in front of a store that sold baby clothing, toys, and food. Once he got near the stroller, he realized a baby was strapped into it. There seemed to be nobody watching it. He casually got on his knees and started talking to the baby and getting her to laugh. Still, nobody came around, so he stood up and walked away with the stroller.

After the baby's mother noticed that the baby and stroller were missing, she and some store employees began looking all over with no luck. They called the police, who helped in the search, and an hour later, they found the stroller on a street in front of an apartment building, but the baby was gone. Two officers buzzed the apartment building manager, and she let them in. They wanted to talk to each resident to see if they noticed anything. Walking down the hallway to the landlady's apartment, they noticed a small bundle of clothing lying on the floor. Once they approached it, they realized that it was the missing baby and, sadly, the infant was dead.

Only three days later, Anatoly was crossing the downtown streets again, looking for another child victim. Like the first baby he abducted and murdered, he found another stroller parked out in front of a Children's World Store. Like the first time, he walked up to the baby, talked to it for a while, and then walked away with the baby and stroller without anyone noticing him.

When this happened, police assigned a specific task force to find the missing baby and to start a formal investigation. They needed to know if this was just one particular suspect who was going around stealing and killing babies.

Police found the remains of the second baby, who had gone missing almost a month later, on October 17th. Her little body was found in a landfill on the outskirts of Moscow. This time, the baby had been sexually assaulted.

One week later, Anatoly tried to kill again. He was walking in Chekhov, a suburb of Moscow when he came across another baby strapped into her carriage outside a child's store. Again, he leaned down and began talking to the baby, making it laugh, and when nobody came out of the store, he stood up and began to walk away with the carriage and baby. Not even two minutes later, the mother came running out of the store and started yelling at him.

Anatoly stopped dead, turned around, saw her screaming, and began to panic. Several people were out on the street shopping and doing things around lunchtime, and when they all heard the mother scream, most stopped to look at what was happening. Once Anatoly noticed everyone watching him, he let go of the baby carriage and ran away.

The baby's mother soon caught up to the stroller, grabbed her baby from it, and held her, but kept screaming. Several onlookers began to chase Anatoly down the street, but they were soon out of sight of the mother.

The Baby Store had called the police, who arrived quickly. When the three men who chased Anatoly returned, they told the police that he had escaped from them. But they were able to give a detailed description of him. The description was so thorough that they were able to find him and arrest him that very night.

After the police finished their investigation, they were able to associate him with the three other baby abductions. He was charged with five murders, all with aggravating circumstances— meaning he was abnormally cruel in the way that he had murdered them.

The trial only lasted one week, and he was convicted of all charges and sentenced to death. He appealed the sentence to the Supreme Court, but it was denied. While waiting on death row, he attempted to hang himself in his cell but was discovered before he died.

On February 24, 1979, Anatoly was executed by firing squad in Moscow.

TWENTY-TWO

Nikolay Sakharov

THE VOLOGDA RIPPER

Nikolay Alexandrovich Sakharov was born in Nepotyagovo, Vologda, Soviet Union, on April 22, 1954. His father was injured while fighting in the war and disabled when he returned to the family. He died soon after

Nikolay's birth. His mother worked at a farm to support the family.

Nikolay was a very disciplined and well-structured young man but didn't do well in school. At fifteen, in 1969, he joined the Komsomol – a youth group for the Soviet communist party and military to influence youth to participate as adults. A year later, when he finished the eighth grade, he started working as a tractor driver for the same farm his mother worked on. He quit that job in 1974 to work for the police department in one of their jails but was fired within a year because he was too friendly with the prisoners.

For the next year or so, Nikolay had several odd jobs, which lasted only a month or two until October 1976, when he got a job in a different jailhouse. This time, he was employed as a guard. But again, after only one year, he was fired from this prison for having too many violations.

Throughout these years, he met and married a woman. The marriage ended in divorce after two years because he often had sex with other women he met in bars. A fact that he didn't try to hide from her. After his wife left him, he began to rape and murder different women in town.

In 1977, five girls in the city went missing without a trace. Many rumors started spreading around town, and people were fearful. Even though there were only five missing officially, the story on the street was that dozens of girls had been abducted. True or not, the city was in a panic.

Even though Nikolay knew police were out in large numbers trying to capture the town rapist and murderer, he wasn't scared and continued to look for victims. He would drive around town and look for women walking alone in the city. He would pull over and ask them if they needed a ride somewhere. The women trusted him because he usually wore one of his prison guard uniforms, and the girls believed he was a policeman.

If he decided to rape and kill the woman he picked up, he would drive them out of town into a wooded rural area to rape them. After he was finished, he killed the women by hitting them over the head with a hammer he carried in his car. He would burn their bodies while still in the bush, and once the fire went out, he would smash their skulls into pieces. He would wrap all the remains in a large towel or blanket and dump them in the river. He often took jewelry and watches from his victims and gave them as a gift to other women he was dating.

Once arrested in January 1978, he readily

confessed to having committed three murders in 1977: Tatyana Svetina, Natalia Vinogradova, and Marina Mukhina. He was charged with the three murders, and his trial began on July 18, 1978. It lasted only one week. At the trial, Nikolay admitted to committing the murders and asked not to be put to death, but the court rejected that. He was found guilty and sentenced to death.

On February 5, 1979, he was executed by a firing squad in Moscow.

TWENTY-THREE

Vladimir Tretyakov

THE NURSEMAN OF ARKHANGELSK

Vladimir Nikolaevich Tretyakov was born in Arkhangelsk, USSR, on August 19, 1979. His father left before he was born, and his mother raised him. She was an abusive alcoholic who wasn't at home much because she was out at a bar or meeting men. When she was home, she often ordered Vladimir around, telling him to clean or make her some food or drink. If he made a mistake, she would hit him.

As he grew older, Vladimir couldn't wait to leave his home, and he began to feel hatred towards his mother. This hatred eventually developed into hostility for all women who drank. As soon as he graduated from school, he joined the army. Once his army service was over, Vladimir got married and started working as an apprentice for a butcher. Then, he got a better-paying job on the railway. His wife also liked to drink. Every time he was home with her, she would get drunk. It reminded him of his mother, and the couple would fight about it. It wasn't long before his wife asked him to leave their house.

Vladimir decided to move, and in 1975, his position was transferred to the city of Arkhangelsk. While there, he was promoted to railway engineer and volunteered for the local branch of the People's Guard, a group of civilians that tried to help law enforcement control crime in the area. He became well-known in town and often helped catch criminals and thieves. His good reputation got him a promotion and an apartment in a brand-new building in the city.

In 1977, Vladimir met and started dating Angelina Koroleva. The two became very serious quickly, and she stayed at his apartment every night. But as his girlfriends and wife before her, Angelina drank alcohol as well. His dislike of her drinking caused the couple to argue. He had no tolerance for alcohol, and he didn't want her to drink at all, not even one drink.

On December 9th that year, Vladimir returned home from work and found Angelina drunk, almost to the state of being passed out. He became so enraged that he strangled her to death. Later, when he calmed down, he decided to cut her up into pieces to dispose of her body. He packed her cut-up remains in his backpack and went to a vacant parking lot in an abandoned area of town where he disposed of them. He went there every night for a week, dumping the pieces at night until he had gotten rid of every trace of her.

After this was done, he began to believe that it was his duty or job to rid the city of women who were drunks or alcoholics. And he immediately started his quest. He planned first to find a drunk woman, then follow her home and kill her.

Within days, on December 13th, Vladimir killed Petrova S. after watching her out at a bar alone, getting drunk. When she left, he followed her to her apartment. When she entered her apartment, he forced his way in and strangled her to death. He then cut her body up into pieces and, like before, dumped her remains in abandoned parking lots or buildings over several trips, using his backpack to carry the pieces.

That month, he repeated this process with two other women: Anna Popova and Ekaterina Marchenko. Then, the following month, January 1978, three more murders: Maria Gerasimova, Inna Ignakhina, and Sveta Eremeeva.

Vladimir's girlfriend was reported missing, and the police went to his apartment to ask him about it. He had no good answers for them, so they took him to the police station for further questioning while his apartment was searched. Under interrogation, Vladimir ended up confessing to seven murders. He even brought the police to each spot where he left their remains. His psychiatric examination diagnosed him as having psychopathy, but he was still fit to stand trial.

Vladimir was found guilty of all charges, and on August 30, 1978, he was sentenced to death. He made two appeals to the sentence, claiming that it was because of his lousy childhood that he killed the women. Both appeals were denied. On August 19, 1979, Vladimir was executed by firing squad.

TWENTY-FOUR

Vladimir Storozhenko

THE SMOLENSK STRANGLER

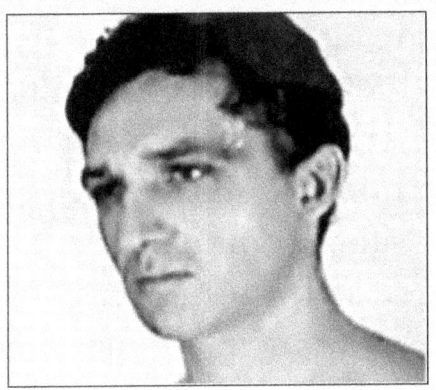

Vladimir Viktorovich Storozhenko was born in Smolensk, Soviet Union, on April 11, 1953. While growing up, he often got into trouble with the police for small thefts and hurting his neighbor's pets. The girls in school tried to avoid him as he was always very aggressive towards them in a sexual manner. He only went to school until eighth grade, and then after that, he quit so he could work.

Over the next two years, he was arrested and convicted two different times: once for rape, and he was placed in jail for two years because he was still a minor, and then for breaking into an apartment where he stole some money.

After he was released from serving his time for both crimes, he got a job as a driver, met a woman, married, and the couple had a son. He even began to gain a good reputation around his neighborhood for being a good father and doing his job well. He was now entering his early twenties, and it looked like he was settling into an everyday life without crime.

In 1978, a series of at least twenty attacks were made on women around Smolensk. The attacks continued for the next three years. Of all the women who were attacked, thirteen of them were sexually assaulted and then murdered. The city of Smolensk panicked, and the media reported on the attacks daily. Several suspects were brought in and questioned. Anybody who had any record of sexual assaults was watched closely. Some suspects were even charged in some cases and ended up in jail for months until the real culprit, Vladimir Storozhenko, was apprehended.

In 1981, Vladimir's last victim survived her attack and was able to give a good description of her rapist, including a large tattoo on his chest. She identified him from his photo.

Police arrested Vladimir and brought him in for questioning. They ran his blood sample on one of the victims who scratched her attacker, and it matched. When police searched Vladimir's apartment, they found some of the victim's jewelry and personal items. His wife said they were a birthday gift from her husband. They had initially belonged to one of his victims.

After he was presented with all this evidence, Vladimir confessed to his crimes. He was charged and convicted of thirteen murders, all with aggravating circumstances. He was convicted after a trial and sentenced to death. After two failed appeals of his sentence, he was executed by firing squad on September 22, 1982. His brother Sergei was also charged and convicted of criminal conspiracy for helping Vladimir with helping conceal the crimes and sentenced to fifteen years in prison.

TWENTY-FIVE

Vasily Smirnov

THE NECROMANCER

Vasily Alexandrovich Smirnov was born in Sopka, Tver, Soviet Union, on November 30, 1947. He was an only child, and his father died before he was in school. His mother was very conservative and strict with him, so much so that he was not only not allowed to go to any school dances or events, but he was also forbidden to talk to other classmates unless necessary, and only boys.

When he was eighteen years old, and after he completed school, he got into an argument with his mother, which led him to attack her with a hammer. As the fight worsened, he ripped her clothing off and tried to rape her, but she was able to fight him off. She decided not to call the police because she didn't want to lose him or see him go to jail.

After the assault on his mother, Vasily promised never to do it again and joined the army at her request. She thought the military would straighten him out and put him on the right path. But while serving, he was accused of raping an older woman he had met on the streets when he was on break. He was arrested, charged, and convicted of the rape and was sent to prison for six years.

During his time in prison and because he was in for raping an older woman, he was not well-liked and often poorly treated. His cellmate continuously raped and tortured him. He was offered around to several other prisoners who raped and beat him as well. The guards were uninterested in helping him and often looked the other way.

He could only report it to his mother, who said she would do something about it when she visited him. Only soon after that first visit his mother died.

After he was released from prison, he worked on a farm as a cattle slaughterer. It wasn't long before victims of sexual assault and or murder began to appear. On September 3, 1979, eight-year-old Marina Koshkina washed up on the banks of the Izora River. After a medical examination, it was determined that she had had a nail hammered into her head as well as being sexually assaulted. A considerable panic came over the city, and police added reinforcements to walk the streets regularly.

Less than a month after the discovery of Marina's body, the body of a young five-year-old boy, Andrei Lopatin, was found dead on the shores of Silver Lake. The boy had been raped and then stabbed to death. Later, after Vasily was captured, he told police that he also wanted to cut off a piece of the boy's flesh for food, but a cyclist came along and frightened him away before he could do it.

After the murders of these two children were

discovered and the way they had been killed, many rumors circulated that it was a vampire or some kind of creature going around town looking for children's blood to drink.

Vasily also claimed that he was not out looking for victims to kill. He just wanted to have sex with them. But after he raped them, if they wouldn't agree to tell anyone, he had to kill them. So, in his mind, it was the victim's fault for their death.

Vasily next went to work for an older, well-off woman in the neighborhood to do some work for her. Instead, once he was let into her house, he hit her over the head with a shovel he was using to dig up some ground on her property. After that, he stabbed the woman to death before removing her head with his shovel. He robbed her, and then he set her house on fire.

With so much media and police presence, he headed to a different town, Petergof. Once there, he met a pregnant woman who he raped. Because she agreed not to go to the police, he didn't kill her. After the attack, Vasily wasn't comfortable staying in that town. He thought she might tell someone, so he went to another town, Gachina.

While in Gachina, he decided to go to a seminar about finding work. He met a teacher who was also a mother of two children. After the event was over, he raped and killed her. After her murder gained so much attention, he decided that he would stop attacking people and go into hiding for a while.

One of Vasily's rape victims went to police and told them about the assault. Police realized that Vasily had been in jail before for similar crimes, so they went to his residence to bring him in for questioning. When police arrived at his place, they found the inside had been burned out.

A week later, Vasily went to a schoolyard where several children played. He went into a rage and started to grab the children and rip their clothes off. He raped one of them, but several went back into the school, where police were called. He was arrested.

Under interrogation, Vasily proudly admitted to his rapes and murders and also claimed that with each of his victims, he would hammer a nail into their heads before leaving them.

Vasily was charged with five counts of murder and convicted on all counts. He was sentenced to death. He was executed by firing squad in an unknown location in Moscow and on an unknown date in 1980.

TWENTY-SIX

Anatoly Nagiyev

THE MAD ONE

A natoly Huseinovich Nagiyev was born in Angarsk, Irkutsk, Soviet Union, on January 26, 1958. His father got a job in Sudzha, so the whole family, including his two sisters, moved there shortly after his birth. Anatoly was a natural in sports and became a gymnast while in school. He was quite a bit shorter than most others in his age group, and girls often made fun of him. As a result, he became withdrawn from people.

Just around the time when he was graduating from school, in May and June 1975, he sexually assaulted three different girls, all from his school, on three different occasions. He was arrested, charged, and convicted on all three charges and sentenced to six years. He was released on parole for good behavior after only serving three years.

Anatoly decided to move to Chikshino and started to work there. On January 30th, while he was on his way home, he met a lady, Olga Demyanenko, on the streets of downtown. For some reason, she invited him to her apartment. There, he raped and killed her.

On May 28th, Anatoly was taking a train home from work and met a woman, Daria Kravchenko. She was on the train because her car had broken down. During the trip, he managed to rape and murder her. Somehow, he managed to stuff her body into the luggage compartment, which was located beneath their seats on the train, without anyone noticing. Once her body was discovered on the train, there were several news articles about both killings. He decided to move to Kursk, where he got a job working as a projectionist at a movie theatre.

On July 4, 1980, Anatoly took a train heading to Moscow. While he was on that train, he managed to sexually assault and murder four different women on four other occasions. From each of his victims, he stole any money and jewelry they had. While he was committing his crimes, two different passengers walked in on him, so he killed both of them as well. Two different train employees also happened upon him while he was committing his crimes, so he murdered them. He threw each victim out a window between station stops.

Detectives created a list of several items that were stolen or reported missing from the bodies on the train by their relatives. These lists were sent to all the pawn shops in the area in case someone tried to sell any items.

Anatoly gave one of his victims' rings to a friend. This friend pawned the ring, and the pawn shop dealer reported it to the police. When police questioned the man who sold the ring, he told them that he got it from Anatoly.

Police arrived at Anatoly's house and

conducted a search. They ended up finding a notepad containing a list of several of the victims' addresses. On September 12, 1980, Anatoly was arrested.

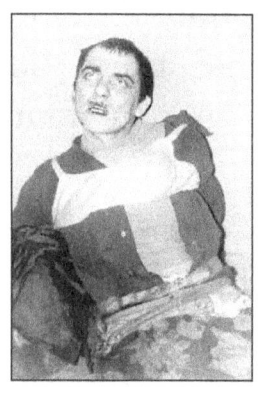

After a few months of interrogations, he admitted to all his crimes. He was charged and convicted of eight murders. He was then sentenced to death and sent to death row at Novocherkassk. After he arrived at the prison, he managed to escape. It took law enforcement two months to finally catch him on a farm where he was disguised as a traveling gypsy.

During his arrest, police shot him several times. He was taken to a hospital, where they managed to fix him. He was executed by firing squad on October 28, 1981.

TWENTY-SEVEN

Nikolai Fefilov

THE URAIS STRANGLER

Nikolai Borishovich Fefilov was born sometime in 1946 in Sverdlovsk, USSR, and not much is known about his childhood or family while he was a child. We do know that he joined the army in 1965 and was demobilized the following year. He then got a job as a printer apprentice for the town newspaper.

While working at the newspaper, he met the woman he later married, with whom he had two daughters. Things were hard for his family as they could only afford to live in a communal setting, where they shared their bathroom with other tenants. His wife frequently argued with Nikolai because she wanted him to get a better job so they could move into a better place. The couple's fights would get nasty, and Nikolai never made it more than a few hours before he left the house in a rage. Often, he wouldn't return until after it was dark.

On one of these occasions, April 29, 1982, after he left the house, Nikolai drove around the Verkh-Isetsky town district. When passing a bus stop, he noticed a young girl, Lena Mangusheva. She was a fifth-grade school girl, probably about ten years old, sitting alone at the stop, and it was well past school starting time. He pulled over, got out of his car, and talked with her. He offered her a ride.

Once he got her alone, he sexually assaulted her and strangled her to death with his tie. He took her body to a local park and dumped it there, covering her up with branches and logs. He took her school bag and removed the pencil case and the textbooks before disposing them in a gas station washroom.

The next day, Lena's body was discovered by a couple out walking in the park. Police immediately began to focus on anybody who was living in the area and those who had sexual offenses on their records. The detective's primary suspect was Georgy Khabarov, a twenty-eight-year-old mentally disabled man who had been in prison for a robbery and an attempted rape.

When they first questioned him, he claimed he was at home all day, not going out. But on his second interrogation, Georgy broke down and told them that he had raped and murdered the girl. The only thing was that he got all of the details wrong. The location of where the rape and murder happened was wrong, and he said that he stabbed the girl to death after the rape. He also gave the wrong description of the girl's appearance and hair color. The medical examiner determined that Georgy did not have the correct blood type as it didn't match the sperm that was left on the girl's body.

Even with the mistakes that Georgy made in his confession and no physical evidence linking him to the murder, he was arrested, charged, and on September 24, 1982, put on trial for the rape and murder of Lena. He was also charged with a second attempted rape of a different woman and an assault on a third victim. The court found him guilty of Lena's murder and sentenced him to a term in prison of fourteen years.

After imprisonment, he filed an appeal against his conviction, stating all of the mistakes made at the trial. At the same time, the mother of the murdered child, Lena, also filed an appeal to the court asking that Georgy be sentenced to death for the murder because fourteen years was not a fair sentence.

The Supreme Court ruled on both appeals, saying the conviction should be canceled and a new trial be held in a different jurisdiction. He was retried in the Spring of 1983, and on March 23rd, the Sverdlovsk Court found Georgy guilty of Lena's murder. This time, he was sentenced to death. A month later, on April 27th, he was executed by firing squad.

Even with all the media sensation Georgy's trial had, Nikolai would kill again. On August 7, 1983, while Georgy was sitting on death row, Nikolai murdered and raped twenty-two-year-old Guinara Yakupova. He spotted her at a bus stop on her way home from college and offered her a ride home. He strangled her with his belt after raping her. He dumped her body in the bush surrounding the local stadium. He later admitted to returning to the crime scene and spending time with her corpse at least three times after the murder and before she was found on October 7th.

Police interviewed Guinara's schoolmates, friends, and family and learned that she had been having problems with an old boyfriend named Mikhail Titov. Titov had been arrested for sexually harassing other girls that he didn't know, and to make things worse for him, police learned that he was an outpatient at a mental clinic.

Nikolai's next victim was another fifth-grade girl named Natasha Lapshina on May 11, 1984. After picking his victim up at the bus stop, his attack was much more brutal than his previous ones. Not only was Natasha raped and strangled, but he removed all of her clothing and inserted a stick in her vagina. He then dumped her body in a ditch that was three-quarters full of dirty water. He also removed the contents of her school bag and dumped all her clothing along deserted back roads outside of town. Her body was found the following day.

Under pressure from the public, the police would go back to Titov and arrest him for both murders. During his interrogations, he told different stories each time. The locations of where the murders happened or where the bodies were found were never correct. But the police were persistent. They came up with witnesses to say that they had seen Titov at the locations of both murders on the correct dates. So, he was arrested and sent to prison.

Later, he was admitted to the hospital for the injuries he had received from the police during his questioning about the cases. He died about two months later from these injuries. The detective who was in charge of his interrogations was fired after his death. Police assigned both murders to Titov and closed both cases.

The following year, on May 6, 1985, Nikolai decided to spend the afternoon at a local lake. While there, he noticed Lansa Dyachuk, a twenty-one-year-old medical student, lying on the beach reading. He approached her, and they had a conversation for a while. Later, after all the other people left, he attacked her, sexually assaulted her, and strangled her to death. He also inserted a large stick in her vagina and scattered all of her clothing around the beach. Before leaving, he took some of her jewelry, a watch, and a scalpel that the girl had. Nikolai did not attempt to hide the body in any way. Her body was not found until almost two weeks later, on May 17th. A few different suspects were arrested, and one of them was tried two times for the murder but not convicted.

On May 26, 1986, Olga Timofeeva was walking near the town's stadium when Nikolai jumped out of the bushes and surprised her. He strangled her to death before sexually assaulting her. This time, he mutilated her body even more than the last two victims. He not only inserted a stick in her vagina, but he also cut and removed her breasts. Again, he would remove her jewelry and cover her body with branches. Her body was found two days later.

After the murder of Olga Timofeeva, the senior detectives on the case started connecting all of the murders. They would then create a specific task force dedicated to the rapes and murders to try and solve these cases and stop the killings.

With all of the new police attention around the bus stops and stadium where Nikolai had found his previous victims, he decided that he would go to a different location to find possible victims. On May 22, 1987, he started hanging around the Zheleznodorozhny District near the train station. That day, he saw nineteen-year-old Elena Kook leaving the station. He grabbed her and strangled her until she passed out. Then, he took her to a private location and sexually assaulted her before choking her to death with his belt. He also cut off her breasts and inserted a branch in her vagina before throwing her body into the bushes located behind the train station. Her body was found the next day, and as before, police rounded up the known sexual offenders. Three of the suspects that police detained confessed to the murder.

About one year later, on April 25, 1988, Nikolai was searching the Mayakovsky Central Park in the Oktabrsky District for a possible victim when he came across a young woman who was cutting through the park on her way home after work. He sexually assaulted and strangled her to death. Like the victims before her, he took her jewelry and money before trying to hide the body. Only this time, while he was shoving her body into a pile of brush and covering it with branches, a police lieutenant, Yevgeny Mordvyanik, happened to be walking by the area and spotted him. Nikolai was arrested on the spot.

In police custody, it wouldn't take long before he began to confess all of the sexual assaults and murders, including the cases where police had accused others. Georgy Khabarov, who had been convicted and executed for the murder and rape of Lena Mangusheva, had his conviction canceled posthumously.

Nikolai was charged with seven murders, and the trial date was set. The reputation of the police was now terrible for making so many mistakes, accusing the wrong people of the crimes, and allowing the murders to continue. The trial was expected to be a scandal for police. But the night of August 30th, the night before the trial was to begin, Nikolai was murdered by his cellmate.

The criminal case was terminated after Nikolai's death was discovered. No law enforcement officers were disciplined for any of their procedures during the investigation of Nikolai.

TWENTY-EIGHT

Andrei Chikatilo

THE BUTCHER OF ROSTOV

Andrei Romanovich Chikatilo was born in Yabluchne, Sumy, Ukraine on October 16, 1936. His parents were farmers who lived in a one-bedroom shack. Ukraine was recovering from a severe famine induced by Stalin, during which millions of Ukrainians died. At that time, none of the farmers were being paid any wages. They were allowed to plant and live off some of what they grew.

It was also a time of fear for children like Andrei. His mother had always told him to be careful, as his older brother, Stephan, had been abducted at the age of four and eaten by starving neighbors of theirs. There has never been any official record of an older brother named Stephan being born to his parents, but Andrei believed it happened.

Things became even more challenging for his family after the Soviet Union entered World War II. His father was conscripted into the army and had to leave their home to go and fight with the Red Army. In late 1941, his father was hurt in battle and later captured by the Nazis.

Life around Andrei's home worsened as bombings became the norm for the area, and Nazi troops came through the area, shooting people on the streets. They were often forced out of their home and had to hide in ditches or the woods. Later, their house was burned by Nazi troops.

Often, the Nazi soldiers raped women they

came across, which is likely what happened to Andrei's mother in 1943 when she became pregnant and gave birth to a girl named Tatyana.

At the end of the war, Andrei went back to school. He loved to read both at school and at home. But he often became faint throughout the day because the country was still experiencing a post-war famine. In 1950, just after he turned fourteen, he became the school newspaper editor. At sixteen, he became the Chairman of the Communist Party Committee for School Children, organizing marches and meetings. He graduated from school in 1954 with above-average grades.

Andrei applied to the University of Moscow, and despite his excellent grades, he was turned down. He blamed his father for the rejection because his father was considered a traitor after the enemy captured him during battle. He didn't apply to any other universities but instead decided to travel.

Andrei ended up in Kursk, where he got a job as a laborer. He started dating a woman he met there. Over the next eighteen months, he attempted to have sex with his girlfriend but was unable to maintain an erection. Eventually, they separated.

After this, he got a construction job at a site in Nizhny Tagil. Andrei stayed there for almost two years until he was drafted into the military in 1957. During his three years of service, he guarded the country's borders with Central Asia. When his service ended, he returned to where his family was and farmed there.

He started dating an older divorced woman for about three months, but they would also break up because of his impotence. The woman told several acquaintances of theirs about why they broke up, and this embarrassed Andrei so much that he tried to hang himself. He was found by his mother and a neighbor, who pulled him down.

About seven months later, Andrei moved to Rostov to work as a communications engineer. When his younger sister Tatyana graduated from school, she moved into his apartment with him. Within six months, she married a man and moved in with her new husband at his parent's place. But while she was still living with her brother, she introduced him to a friend of hers, Feodosia Odnacheva, and they married within two weeks of meeting in 1963. The couple had a daughter, Lyudmila, in 1965 and a son, Yuri, in 1969. During that time, Andrei took correspondence courses at Rostov University to obtain his language and philosophy degree, and he became a teacher in those subjects in 1970.

Andrei was well-versed in the subjects he taught but was not good at controlling his classroom, and his students often made fun of him. Andrei ensured that the students living on campus were checked in by nighttime. The students knew he often came into the girls' rooms, hoping to see them undressed. Later, he told the police that he used to come across students having sex, and it would bother him because they could do what he always wished he could but was unable to.

The first known sexual assault by Andrei took place in May 1973. In the pool, he saw a young student he had found attractive. He stood up to her and put one arm around her while, with his other hand, grabbed her breasts and genitals. As the student fought to get away from him, he ejaculated in his shorts and let her go. The incident was not reported at the time.

Two months later, he asked a female student to remain after class. Thinking she was in trouble, she waited until everyone else left the room to ask what she had done wrong. He closed and locked the door to the classroom. He walked over to her and began to hit her until she fell to the ground.

He sexually assaulted her by grabbing different parts of her body and ejaculating in his pants before letting her leave. This incident also went without Andrei being disciplined.

Andrei was known for playing with himself through his pants while fully clothed and watching some of his students. Not only did students catch him doing this, but other teachers at the school as well.

Eventually, these incidents started to be reported to the administration. After enough complaints were lodged, the school's director scheduled a formal interview with Andrei. It was decided that he should resign. If he didn't resign, they would fire him. And why he was fired would become public.

Andrei decided it would be better for him to quit the job, so he did. In less than three months, in January 1974, he got another job as a teacher in a school in Novoshakhtinsk. That job lasted four years until September 1978, when the school made some staff cutbacks, and he was laid off.

Andrei next found a job teaching at a technical school in a mining town about fifty kilometers from Rostov, Shakhty. During these years, instead of watching his students, he went to public washrooms and hung out watching children go to the bathroom. With the boys, it was easy for him to enter the washroom, stand beside them at the urinal, and watch them. But for the girls, he had to offer them some candy or gum and talk to them for a while. Once he gained their trust, he went into the bathroom with them and watched. On at least three different occasions, he sexually assaulted the girls by touching them in their genitalia or breast areas.

In 1981, more complaints from both girls and boys started coming into the technical school's administration. Like the first school he worked in, they scheduled a formal meeting with the director of this school, and they offered him the same deal: either quit quietly, or they would fire him and release the reason why he was fired to the public. Again, he opted to quit.

That same month, he returned to Rostov. This time, instead of applying for a job as a teacher at a school, he got a job as a clerk for a factory that made materials for construction companies. In this job, he was required to travel around the country to buy the factory's raw materials to make the construction materials.

In the Fall of 1978, Andrei moved back to Shakhty, where he ended up with two dwellings: one was an apartment where he lived full-time, and the second was an old house falling apart and in terrible shape. The latter is where he committed his first known murder.

On December 22nd, Yelena Zakotnova, a nine-year-old girl, was walking down the street on her way home from school close to where he owned this old house. When Andrei spotted her, he approached her to offer her some candy, which she gladly accepted. After a short conversation, he talked her into entering his house. There, he tried to rape her but was not able to maintain an erection. He blamed this on the girl because she was struggling and not lying still. So, he began to slap her, then choke her, and finally, he stabbed her to death. He ejaculated while he was stabbing her in the stomach. When he was finished, he threw her body into the Grushevka River. Her body washed up on shore two days later.

Initially, police started looking for suspects who had a previous record of sexual assault and were living in the area. They found twenty-five-year-old Aleksandr Kravchenko, who was working in town in construction and had served time before for the rape and murder of a teenage girl.

When police came to his house, they found some blood spots on his wife's blouse, which matched the blood type of the victim. Aleksandr had an alibi for the afternoon of December 22nd, as he was home all day with his wife and two of his neighbors. Police threatened his wife with a charge of being an accessory and the two neighbors with perjury if they didn't change their statements. After the pressure from the police, they all changed their stories, stating that Aleksandr had left for a while in the afternoon.

Police then confronted him with the new statements, and he ended up confessing to the rape and murder of the nine-year-old girl. He was charged and faced trial for the murder in 1979. At the trial, he pleaded not guilty and told the court that he was forced into the confession by the detectives. He was convicted and sentenced to death. Upon appeal in 1980, the Supreme Court reduced it to a fifteen-year sentence. The family of the nine-year-old victim appealed to the court after the sentence reduction, and it was decided that the court would retry the whole case. In 1983, at the new trial, Aleksandr was convicted again and sentenced to death. In July of that same year, he was executed by firing squad.

Despite all the press and talk around town about Aleksandr's murder trial and appeal, Andrei struck again. On the afternoon of September 3, 1981, when leaving the library, he noticed Larisa

Tkachenko, a seventeen-year-old student, waiting for a bus. He struck up a conversation with her, and they got along well. She agreed to go with him to the park near the Don River.

When they arrived at the park, he led her to a secluded area, telling her he had some vodka and they could drink some there. Once they reached the spot, he threw her down to the ground, ripped off her clothing, and tried to rape her. Again, he was unable to achieve an erection. During the attack, she began screaming, so he scraped mud off the ground and started to fill her mouth with it to muffle the noise. She continued to fight him, so he strangled her to death.

After that, he was so angry that he started to mutilate her body with a stick of wood he found. He bit off her left nipple. He then covered her body with branches and brush from the area. Her body was discovered the next day.

Nine months after that murder, on June 12, 1982, Andrei took a bus to go shopping for some fresh vegetables in the Bagayevsky District of Rostov. When he got off the bus and started walking towards the market, he ran into Lyubov Biryuk, a thirteen-year-old girl walking home. They started talking, and he ended up accompanying her home.

As soon as they got out of sight of any of the businesses, he jumped on the girl with his whole body weight, which made her fall to the ground and lose her wind. He dragged her into the woods, ripped her dress off, and stabbed her to death. He then covered her in brush and left.

Two weeks later, her body was discovered, and upon a medical exam of her body, it was determined that he had stabbed her a total of twenty-two times in her head, neck, chest, and pelvic area. Some of her injuries in the skull came from the back of her head, suggesting that he stabbed her from behind. The knife had even reached the girl's eye sockets.

This attack, for some reason, seemed to have released any remaining inhibitions Andrei had to commit rape and murder. Over the Summer of 1982, he committed another five murders where his victims were all between the ages of nine and eighteen. His MO of attack and murder in each case was the same. Each victim was lured from a bus stop or train station to a secluded wooded area where they were strangled and stabbed to death after an attempted rape.

On December 11, 1982, Andrei was riding another bus and met Olga Stalmachenok, a ten-year-old girl taking the bus home. Somehow, he talked her into getting off the bus at a stop before she reached her home. He walked her into a farm that had a cornfield and attempted to rape her. He stabbed her over fifty times, completely ripping open her chest, uterus, and bowels. Police questioned some of the other passengers who were on the bus and got their first good description of Andrei.

In January 1983, Moscow decided to send Major Mikhail Fetisov and a task force of ten detectives to Rostov to investigate and solve these murders. The task force was named "Operation Forest Path." They were able to link several of the murders to one killer. After the media reported about the new police task force being in town, Andrei stopped his attacks until the Summer of that year.

Andrei murdered and attempted to rape five more victims over the Summer starting in June. A fifteen-year-old American girl, Laura Sarkisyan, had been visiting her relatives in Rostov. Law enforcement had linked all five of these new attacks to the previous ones because of the pattern of the killer.

One theory about the murders was that it was a satanic panic. In the 1980s, America was going through what was called the "Satanic Panic," and soon, this title was attached to all of these recent murders in the Soviet Union. Police began to think that this was some satanic cult who were probably harvesting body organs.

At the same time, other detectives believed a different theory. They felt that the killer was a homosexual with a mental illness. During this time, the two were considered to be connected. Three known and convicted homosexuals were interrogated so vigorously and abusively by police that they later committed suicide.

In 1984, Andrei continued his murder spree in Rostov, starting with two more women in the Park of Aviators. In late March, he spotted a ten-year-old boy in Novoshakhtinsk at a kiosk and talked the boy into going for a walk with him into the woods. The boy's body was discovered three days later. He had been sexually assaulted and stabbed to death.

During their investigation, police talked to several witnesses who could describe the man seen walking away with the boy. They created a composite drawing of him and passed it around. Police also acquired a semen sample and a footprint of the killer.

Two months later, on May 25th, Tatyana Petrosyan was walking through the park with her ten-year-old daughter just outside Shakhty when they ran into Andrei. He attacked and killed both of them. Over the next two months, June and July, he killed three more people in the same park, including two teenage girls and a thirteen-year-old boy.

In August, Andrei decided to change the location of his murders, so he returned to the Park of the Aviators. On August 2nd, he lured and murdered Natalya Golosovskaya, a sixteen-year-old girl, and on the 7th, he murdered seventeen-year-old Lyudmila Alekseyeva. Both suffered severe knife wounds and were dumped into the river. Later in August, the body of an eleven-year-old boy washed up on the river bank in the park. He had been castrated and had his eyes removed from his face.

On September 13, 1984, Andrei was spotted by two undercover detectives at a bus stop in Rostov. He was apparently just hanging around talking to any young girl who would respond to him. After he didn't connect with any of them, he began walking away from the stop and towards the downtown area.

While walking the streets, he approached several women, stopping and talking with them while seemingly touching himself. The detectives watched him do this for several hours before arresting him.

Once he was arrested, they searched him and found an eight-inch knife, several ropes, and a jar of Vaseline on him. Some of the other detectives at the police station had been investigating Andrei for a minor theft that he had committed with a former employer. This allowed them to hold him in custody for a few days while investigating him further.

Detectives took a sample of Andrei's blood, and it was determined to be blood type A, but the six semen samples from the victims that police had were all from a suspect with blood type AB. Detectives started to think that he wasn't the culprit they were looking for.

Andrei was convicted of the theft of his former employer, though, and sentenced to serve one year in prison. He was released after only three months on December 12, 1984. By this time, the task force had positively linked twenty-three of the murders together as being committed by the same person.

Andrei moved to Novocherkassk and got a job working in the supply department of a train factory. He was trying hard not to attract the attention of any detectives or police. He wouldn't murder again until August, eight months after his release from prison.

While traveling to Moscow for work, he met Natalia Pokhlistova, an eighteen-year-old student who was also taking a train to Moscow. After a short conversation, they exited the train and walked through the forest towards Vostryakovo. Once in the bush, he tied her up, attempted to rape her, and stabbed her thirty-eight times, mainly in her neck and chest.

Three weeks later, Andrei struck again. This time, he attacked Irina Gulyaeva, who was also riding the train, and like his earlier victim, he was lured from the train and into the woods and, after tying her up, raped and stabbed her to death.

The special task force created to find this serial killer had now expanded to twenty-one officers. They had also added a psychiatrist to try and profile who the serial killer might be. In the following year, 1987, Andrei killed three times: twelve-year-old Oleg Makarenkov on May 12th and twelve-year-old Ivan Bilovetsky in July. These murders were committed in Chikatilo, and therefore, they weren't connected to the serial killer of Rostov. On September 12th, he murdered a sixteen-year-old student, Yuri Tereshonok. As with his previous murders, each of his victims he met either on a train or in a train station.

In 1988, Andrei murdered three more victims: an unidentified female near Krasny Sulin in April, nine-year-old Aleksey Voronko in May, and fifteen-year-old Yevgeny Muratov in July. With all three of these victims, he had gone back to mutilating their bodies with the knife that he used to kill them and his teeth by biting off parts of their bodies. Police also discovered that the knife wounds matched that of three of their other murders and, therefore, linked them to the serial killer that the task force was looking for.

In 1989, Andrei killed five more times. His first victim that year was sixteen-year-old Tatyana Ryzhova, and after he murdered her, he dismembered her body and put the remains in a sewer. This change in MO initially made the police think that it was not a connected murder to the serial killer that they were looking for. The other four victims were killed during the Summer, and only two of these were linked to the killer.

The following year, 1990, Andrei murdered two young boys: eleven-year-old Andrei Kravchenko in January and ten-year-old Yaroslav Makarov in March. Both victims were castrated and stabbed at least fifty times each. Even though the pressure had increased with more police patrols on the streets and at the train and bus stations, he managed to kill three more people that year. By October 1990, they had assigned three hundred and sixty officers to the case.

On November 6, 1990, Andrei met twenty-two-year-old Svetlana Korostik at the Donleskhoz Train Station, luring her into the nearby woods. There, he strangled her and stabbed her to death. But this murder got him noticed. After the murder, Andrei returned to the station. An undercover officer who had noticed him leaving with a girl saw him return alone. The officer walked closer to Andrei and noticed a red smear on his face and dirty elbows on his jacket. It was mushroom picking season in the area, but Andrei was too well-dressed to be picking mushrooms. The officer still thought he looked suspicious, so he checked his papers.

Finding nothing wrong, he let Andrei leave. When the officer returned to the police station, he wrote a report about Andrei and said that he was checked because of a blood smear on his face. About ten days later, the murdered girl's body was found. Because she was found near that train station, headquarters asked the undercover officer who worked at that station to go through every person who was stopped at the train station for the week before the murder. Among the names was Andrei's, so they did a further background check on him.

Investigators were able to place him either living or working in each of the towns where murders occurred and at the same time that they happened. Detectives started to check with the old employers, including the schools that Andrei had taught. They learned that he was asked to leave because he was sexually assaulting the students.

By November 14th, police started a comprehensive surveillance on Andrei. While watching him, they found that he spent a lot of his time traveling the trains. And while on the trains, he often approached young women or children and started talking with them. On November 20th, when Andrei left his apartment carrying a jar full of beer and heading to the park, he was finally arrested.

After his arrest, Andrei stated that the police had made a mistake in arresting him, just as they did back in 1984. Police performed a medical examination on him, and one thing of significance was one of his fingers had a wound on it. Upon further examination, it was determined that it was a human bite.

More evidence was discovered when they searched his possessions and found that he was carrying a knife with him along with two ropes. While the police were doing further investigations on him, he was detained and kept in a cell. Along with him in his cell, they placed what appeared to be another prisoner, but he was an informant. They began to interrogate him the following day. According to Soviet law, they only had ten days to hold him without charging him.

Andrei's second blood test returned, and it was determined that he was type AB, unlike the first time when they tested his blood, where they believed he was type A. So, now his blood type matched the serial murderer.

Throughout the interviews, he claimed that he was innocent of doing any murders or physically assaulting anyone. He did admit to having touched people and even molesting students when he was a teacher years earlier.

It was another whole week of interrogations before Andrei confessed to his crimes. After they brought in the task force psychiatrist to talk with him, about two hours later, he began to cry and started to admit to his murders.

The following day, Andrei formally confessed to thirty-six murders, giving police the details that they needed to charge him with the crimes. He denied two murders that had been linked to the serial killer. He then created a complete, detailed list of each of his victims, along with the location where he murdered them and where he left the bodies. Police even got him to draw pictures of his victims and what the crime scene looked like.

Interestingly, when he was asked why he was cutting the eyes out from his victims in the later murders, he told police that he had heard that the victim's eyes could record the image of the murderer and that it would be possible one day for doctors to get those images and print them off in a picture.

As for the body parts that Andrei had cut or bit off of his victims, he claimed that he just threw the body parts away and that he had only eaten one of his victims' nipples and another victim's tongue.

Andrei was formally charged with thirty-six murders on November 30, 1990. But over the next week, he admitted to killing twenty more people who had never been connected to the serial murderer because either they happened too far away from Rostov or they weren't committed in the same style.

In a few of the murder cases where other

people had been suspected, charged with, or even convicted of the attacks and murder, Andrei provided them with great details and even led them to the remains to prove that he was the one who committed the act.

Andrei also told police about some of the killings they knew nothing about. He admitted to killing a fourteen-year-old boy when he was in Siberia back in 1982. Eventually, he admitted to having committed fifty-six murders, and three of them could not be identified.

After he was formally charged, police sent Andrei to the Serbsky Institute for a six-day mental evaluation in Moscow. They diagnosed him with having prenatal brain damage, which caused him to have different physiological issues. He also had a borderline personality disorder with sadistic tendencies, but he was still able to stand a murder trial.

When Andrei was finally brought to trial on April 14, 1992, he was charged with fifty-three murders and five charges of sexual assault on a minor, which had been committed years before when he was a teacher. The trial would be the first murder trial to become a significant media event after the Soviet Union had disbanded and the new freedom began in the country. The relatively new freedom of the media allowed them to go wild, and they often described the murders in great detail and gave him handles such as "Maniac," "Cannibal," or "Satanic."

It took the first two days of the trial to read out all of the murder charges. It then continued with the details of each of the crimes, including any sexual assault murders. Many people, both inside the courtroom and standing outside the courthouse, were crying and screaming throughout the day. With the media reporting on all of this, the city of Rostov became obsessed and focused on the trial, and so did the whole country.

On May 13th, Andrei withdrew his confession of six of the murders he had earlier confessed to and admitted to committing four other murders that were not linked to this trial. This change led the defense attorney to request that Andrei be sent for a second mental evaluation. The court denied the request. Andrei stopped talking to his lawyer and refused to answer the judge or prosecutor at the trial. The court took a two-week break to figure out how to handle this.

When the trial resumed in July, the doctor who gave Andrei his sixty-day analysis gave testimony, which took three hours. After he was done, four other psychiatrists took the stand to provide the results of all of Andrei's tests that were given during those two months. It was determined that he had committed all of these attacks and could not be excused because of insanity.

On October 14th, the court reached its final decision. It took two days to read the verdict. Andrei was found guilty on fifty-two of the murder charges and not guilty on one. He was also found guilty on five charges of sexual assault on a minor, which he committed during the years that he was a teacher.

The following day, he was sentenced to death plus eight years in prison. When the judge read the sentence, Andrei stood up, swearing loudly, and kicked the defense table across the room.

Andrei appealed to the Supreme Court, but the appeal was denied. He then filed an appeal to President Boris Yeltsin, which was also rejected on January 4, 1994.

On February 14th of the same year, he was taken to a soundproof room located in the Novocherkasek Prison and executed by a single gunshot behind his right ear. He was later buried in an unmarked grave in that same prison cemetery.

TWENTY-NINE

Vasily Kulik

THE MURDER DOCTOR

V asily Sergeyevich Kulik was born in Irkutsk, Soviet Union, on January 17, 1956. His father was a doctor who studied biological sciences and wrote medical papers, and his mother was a school headmistress. He and his two siblings were raised well and had a good standard of living.

Kulik often had loud, angry outbursts for no reason. He was a sleepwalker who would even leave his house while in that state. But the most disturbing characteristic was that he was mean to animals.

Despite his problems, he did well in school and became a boxer, winning the city boxing championship title. This made him popular among his classmates and girls, and he had no problem getting dates.

When Kulik turned eighteen, he served two years of mandatory military service in the Soviet army, finishing in 1976. He then met and married a lawyer, and the couple eventually had children. In the Spring of 1980, when he was walking home, Kulik was attacked by a gang of teenage boys who beat him so severely he had to go to the hospital with bad head injuries.

While he was recovering from his wounds, Kulik wrote a novel in which his main character fell in love and had sex with a nine-year-old girl. Later in his testimony, he told a court that it was during his time in the hospital, when he was healing from his injuries, that he began to have sexual fantasies about young children, both boys and girls. He claimed that he never had them before the attack. He also said that he had become sexually attracted to older females as well.

Once he healed, he began work as a medic for an ambulance service in Irkutsk at their hospital's emergency department. This new job gave him the personal information of the patients who went to the hospital. When he noticed a patient whom he was interested in sexually, he would copy down their addresses and any other information that he needed, go to their home, and then sexually assault and murder them.

In 1984, his first victim was an older woman who had been found on the street unresponsive. After she was taken to the hospital, healed, and returned home, he went to her home, drugged, raped, and strangled her to death.

He continued this pattern of attacks next on an eight-year-old girl and then a fifty-three-year-old woman, who he ended up not only stabbing but shooting to death in her own home. Over the next two years, he would attack, sexually assault, and rape six more children and seven more older ladies from the ages of two years old up to seventy-five.

On January 17, 1986, Kulik was caught

during the act of attacking a woman in her home by the woman's family. They beat him and held him until the police got there. During his interrogations with police, he confessed to all of his murders and was formally charged.

On August 11, 1988, Kulik was convicted of thirteen murders and thirty rapes or sexual assaults. He was sentenced to death. On June 26, 1989, he was executed by a firing squad in Irkutsk.

THIRTY

Sergey Shcherbakov

THE HANDSOME ONE

S ergey Petrovich Shcherbakov was born in the Soviet Union in 1961 or 1962. The exact date or location of his birth is still not known. According to his mother, he was quiet and well-behaved as a child. She lived alone and worked at a factory to support them.

When he graduated from the eighth grade, he entered a vocational school that taught him the technical skills to help him find a job like his mother's. When he completed the two-year course, he entered the army but was quickly dismissed after it was determined he had stolen ammunition from them.

Once he returned home from the military, he discovered that his girlfriend married another man, and he got angry. He moved to Leninsk-Kuzntesky, where he got a job as an electrician in a mine.

While living there, he met a divorced woman, Irina, who was pregnant by her ex-husband. They married. Irina's ex-husband was a prisoner, which is why she divorced him.

Once she had the baby, Sergey seemed angry with her and began fighting with her daily. Things usually ended up with him beating her. He started avoiding going home and would often go out drinking and hang around the streets most nights. Even though Irina thought he was out having an affair with another woman, he was actually getting into fights or attacking random people, beating them up, and stealing something from them.

In 1985, Sergey's violent attacks turned to murder. He started carrying around a hammer in his jacket, some wires he took from his job, or a knife from his kitchen. He would go to the poorest part of town to commit his attacks. He either strangled them, hit them on the head with his hammer, or stabbed them. In the early attacks he committed, he did not rape any of his victims.

His first victim was twenty-seven-year-old pregnant hospital worker Tatiana Berdyugina, whom he murdered when she went out to mail a letter at a mailbox located on the street near her house. After this murder, the local police decided to up the patrol around the area.

Sergey's next murder happened when he spotted the wife of a local tailor, Vera Chulyukova, leaving their business and followed her home. Just before she went inside, he came up behind her and hit her over the head with his hammer. He then robbed her of all the money she carried, which was about ten rubles, some of her jewelry, and a watch. He also took both of the bags she had been carrying.

While Sergey was looking through the woman's bags for valuables, she started coming to.

He dropped the bags, returned to where she was lying, and hit her again with the hammer until she went unconscious again. Then, he grabbed the two bags and left. When her body was discovered, she regained consciousness again and was rushed to the hospital, but died there within a week.

When Vera was first attacked, she let out a loud yell, and one of her neighbors heard her. The neighbor looked out her window but couldn't see anything except what looked like some shadows. She called the police anyway.

During that time, panic hit the streets, and rumors abound of different people being the killer. The only solid thing that the police knew at that time was that it was one person who was committing the murders.

On July 15th, Sergey attacked again. Tatyana Galkina was walking home from work when he surprised her, jumping out of an alley from behind her and stabbing her. She let out a high-pitched scream, which some residents nearby heard, and came out of their homes to see what was happening. Sergey fled from the scene immediately, and Tatyana survived her injuries.

Frustrated, Sergey began to look for another victim. When he noticed fifteen-year-old Vera Kolesnikova walking through Gorky Park, he quickly ran up to her and tackled her with his whole body weight. The weight took her to the ground. He grabbed a handkerchief that he had taken off his victim earlier that day and choked her until she passed out. He then sexually assaulted her and took what he thought was valuable from her purse.

Five days later, when he still hadn't heard any reports about her body being discovered, Sergey decided he would report the murder himself. So, he called the police and told them that he had found a body in the park.

Later that Summer, Sergey saw Ekaterina Lizunova on a construction site go into a trailer on the site. He waited until nobody was around the trailer and then entered it himself. He raped and strangled her to death. After her body was discovered, police found a witness who claimed he saw a man go into her trailer but was unable to give a perfect description because he was too far away to see him.

Sergey then went to the local mine where he had worked before and attacked two more women. With the first one, he grabbed her from behind and tried hitting her with his hammer. But she moved too quickly for him; instead, he hit her shoulder. During their struggle, she grabbed his face and scratched him with her long nails. Surprised, he let go of her and ran away. Some of Sergey's blood and skin remained under her nails, and the police took samples to find out the attacker's blood type.

Sergey then attempted to attack and murder another mine worker. But during their fight, she was able to hit him with a bag full of tools. He fell to the ground, and she was able to run screaming to find help.

Sergey's last known murder happened on September 21st when Elena Muratova was coming home after being out dancing with a female friend. While they were walking, he began to follow them, and when he caught up, he started talking to the two women. He asked Muratova if she wanted to come to his place for a drink, but she said no. The girls walked away, and Sergey began to follow them again, but at a distance.

Once the one girl got to her house, Muratova was on her walk to her place. He ran up to her and began to hit her on the head with his hammer. He raped and killed her and stole her gold watch from her body. Later, Muatova's friend she was walking with identified the man who approached them. She also knew what street he lived on because when he talked to the two women, he told them he was married and where he lived to try and win their confidence.

Police went to the street where Sergey lived and waited to see if a man matching the description they got showed up. Within a day, as he left his house to go to work, the officers noticed him and thought he looked like the guy they were looking for. Once they approached him and saw the scratch marks on his face, they arrested him. When police searched the house, they found many of the stolen items he took from his victims.

Sergey was charged with six murders and later tried. He was convicted and sentenced to death. He appealed the sentence, but it was denied. He was executed by firing squad on September 26, 1988.

THIRTY-ONE

Igor Chernat

THE EVIL SPIRIT OF KAUKJARVI

Igor Chernat was born in Odesa, USSR, sometime in 1961. Very little is known about Chernat's life before he committed several murders. What was discovered was that he went to a technical school to become a professional driver.

In 1985, he joined the Soviet Army and served as an infantry tank driver for the 138th Motor Rifle Brigade Guards in Kamenka. In November of that year, he joined the army. Also, in that year, he began to murder women.

His first murder was an unidentified woman that he would confess to years later after his arrest. She remains unidentified.

Yevgeniya Nazarova was married to a soldier who worked with Chernat. Visiting her husband, who was ill, she arrived at the base and checked in on her way to the barrack's medical unit. Chernat was there to greet her and escort her in to see him. Instead, he took her to a vacant warehouse where he raped and then killed her by strangling her with a fishing line.

In April of that same year, when the mother of another soldier, Viktoria Bykovskaya, came to the base to visit her son and bring him some food, Chernat was the soldier to escort her. Instead of taking her to her son, he took her to a vacant part of the base, raped, and murdered her as well.

In the Summer of that year, Elena Ivanova, wife of another soldier living at the base, visited her husband. Again, Chernat was to be her escort. Like the others, he took her to a deserted area of the base, raped, and killed her.

With all of his victims, he also took anything of value from their purses and off their bodies. Then, when he was on leave, he sold them at a market in the town of Vyborg.

On his last murder, though, another soldier saw him escorting the victim, and he remembered it because he saw the two of them heading out towards the nearby forest. He thought it was weird and reported it. Officers in charge of the investigation brought Chernat in for questioning.

During the interview, he claimed to know nothing about the murdered women.

When he was released, he left the camp and moved to Odessa, where he created fake documents under a different name. Later that month, when police stopped him and realized that his papers were fake, they arrested him.

While he was at the police station being questioned, he confessed to committing the murders at the military base. He was then returned to the military base, where he was charged and tried by a military tribunal.

In September, the Leningrad Military District tribunal sentenced him to the death penalty. In October 1987, he was executed by a firing squad.

THIRTY-TWO

Mikhail Makarov

Mikhail Olegovich Makarov was born in Leningrad, USSR, on March 12, 1962. He was born into an average working-class family. After graduating from eighth grade, he attended a vocational school and joined the Young Communist League. After serving his mandatory military service, he got a job as a machinist in Leningrad.

While living and working there, he met and married a woman and moved in with her parents. He began to hate living there as her parents always looked down on him and called him names. They didn't believe he made enough money to move out and support his wife. Later, when Makarov was arrested for his crimes, he stated that when reading crime magazines or watching crime movies, he often replaced the victims in the story with his wife's parents.

In February 1986, Makarov knew that one of his neighbors was out and their ten-year-old son was at home alone. He knocked on their door, and when the boy answered it, he asked to come in to leave a note for his parents to read when they returned home. After the boy closed the door, he pulled a screwdriver out of his pocket and began to stab the boy in his head and chest. After the boy passed out, he searched the house for money and valuables. While he was doing this, the boy regained consciousness but pretended to be still knocked out or dead. Once Makarov got everything he wanted, he put his cigarette on the boy's arm. The boy didn't move or scream, and Makarov left. He survived but was permanently disabled.

A few months later, on April 7, 1986, Makarov approached another apartment. This time, an eleven-year-old girl was home alone. He talked his way into the apartment, then raped the girl and stabbed her over thirty times with a screwdriver. He also robbed the apartment.

Later that same month, when Makarov was hanging around the apartment building where he lived, he saw an older woman who lived there taking her garbage out. He followed her to her apartment and forced her inside. There, he stabbed her fifty-one times with his screwdriver and left without robbing her place.

Makarov's next murder was just a few weeks later in another apartment building. This time, his victim was five years old, and he used the same pattern to get in. He also raped and killed her with his screwdriver. In this attack, he decided to trash the apartment completely to make it look like a different person did it.

Makarov made a mistake shortly before murdering the child in her apartment. While walking around the apartment building looking for a victim, he knocked on a door, and when a little boy answered, he began telling the boy that he was working for the library. The boy's mother came out of the bedroom, and when he saw her, he ran. They called the police, and the mother was able to give a good description of him.

Another mistake he made was that during his last murder when he was robbing the apartment, he stole a book and sold it to a used bookstore a few days later. The bookstore owner noticed blood on the book's pages, so after Makarov left, he called the police. The police arrived, got the man's information from the bookstore, went to Makarov's apartment, and arrested him.

During his first interview with detectives, Makarov immediately confessed to his crimes. He also took police to where he had hidden everything that he had stolen during his crimes.

On November 27, 1987, he was convicted of three murders and one attempted murder and sentenced to death. He then appealed for a pardon, but that was refused. He was executed by firing squad in 1988.

THIRTY-THREE

Konstantin Cheryomushkin

THE BATAYSK KILLER

K onstantin G. Cheryomushkin was born in Novocherkassk, Rostov, Soviet Union, in 1963. The location and date of his birth are unknown. When he was young, he learned that his father could not have children of his own, so he would let his mother get pregnant by other men they knew. He never found out who his father was, and he became angry and disrespectful to his parents.

By the time he reached his early twenties, he began to kill. His MO was meeting a young woman and offering her a ride somewhere. He would drive them to a location where there was nobody else around and sexually assault her. After that, he would murder her.

After they were dead, he would try to mutilate their bodies in different ways. With two of the victims, he cut off both of their breasts and the external part of the genitalia. The third victim he burned on a stake.

At the same time that Cheryomushkin was killing, Rostov was also under siege from the serial killer Andrei Chikatilo, a.k.a. "The Butcher of Rostov" (See Chapter 28). This made the investigators think that these murders were also by him. Eventually, the police found evidence to show they were dealing with a different murderer.

In early 1989, Cheryomushkin was detained and brought in for questioning. He confessed his three murders to the police. On November 3, 1989, he was found guilty of all three murders and sentenced to death. After two lengthy appeals that were both denied, Cheryomushkin was executed by firing squad in 1993.

THIRTY-FOUR

Yuri Tsiuman

THE BLACK STOCKING KILLER

Yuri Leonidovich Tsiuman was born in Taganrog, Rostov, Soviet Union, on January 30, 1969. Both of his parents were terrible alcoholics who regularly slapped or beat him. They even told him that they were going to kill him one day. Often, the neighbors reported his father for beating Yuri, and at times, he was arrested. But no real punishment was given to him. When he returned from jail, he would be even more angry with his son and beat him again.

One night, Yuri's father died in his bed, probably from alcohol poisoning. The cause of death was not known as his mother didn't call an ambulance or doctor but instead just left him in his bed. Within a week of his father's death, Yuri's mother started going out to the local bars. She would meet different men, bring them home, and have sex with a lot of them. She also made Yuri watch her have sex with these men.

At seventeen, Yuri was going out to bars to drink and pick up women. On Christmas Eve 1986, when he went out, he saw a sixteen-year-old student, Maria, walking to her friend's house. He grabbed her and forced her into an alley, where the two struggled for a while. Biding for time, she told him that he could come over to her apartment as that would be a better place to have sex. She took him to her place, hoping that someone from her family would be home to help her. But everyone had gone out.

Yuri tied her up, strangled her until she lost consciousness, and sexually assaulted her. After finishing the attack, he went through all of her stuff and took her money and whatever he thought he could sell. He then set her apartment on fire before he left. However, the girl survived the attack.

Over the following two years, Yuri enlisted in the Army and served in the missile forces unit. It was unlikely that he had murdered anyone during those times. He completed his two years of service in the Spring of 1989.

In June of that year, Yuri attacked another woman. Like with his first assault, he spotted the woman on the street walking alone and followed her until he got the opportunity to jump her. He took he into an alley and tried to have sex with her but couldn't. He decided to take her home to his apartment and try it again. Once there, he forced her to have oral sex and then tried to have intercourse with her again. But again, he couldn't perform. Frustrated, he took her back onto the streets and let her go. A few days later, a friend of the woman, who knew what he did, started asking for money, or she would go to the police. Instead of paying her, he just left town.

Over the next two years, he continued to attack and rape women. Four of them were killed, and a fifth one survived. His victims all wore black stockings, and the media at first called him the "Black Stocking Killer."

Yuri's luck ran out when he attempted to rape and kill another woman on November 26, 1992. This time, two strangers appeared and stopped him during the attack. They held him down until the police arrived, and he was arrested.

Yuri was eventually charged with four murders and five sexual assaults. He pled guilty to all charges, and on February 11, 1994, he was sentenced to the death penalty. Just after his sentence, the country placed a moratorium on the death sentence, and his sentence was changed to life imprisonment. This was one of the first complete trials to be televised in the Soviet Union.

THIRTY-FIVE

Andrei Sibiryakov

THE ELUSIVE ONE

A ndrei Vladimirovich Sibiryakov was born in Leningrad, Soviet Union, on February 28, 1964. Not much is known about his family or upbringing. He first became known when he was arrested at seventeen years old and charged with what in the Soviet Union they called "Hooliganism." He served just over one year and was released.

Soon after his release from jail, he married. He started working odd jobs in construction, but they would only last for a while. He often got fired because he would not show up for work. It was said that he had no interest in working and didn't look too hard for a job.

Most of the day, he would walk around town or hang out with some friends because he was too scared to tell his wife that he didn't have a job. On one of those days, when he was walking around, he came across the grave of the infamous Rasputin. The encounter somehow inspired him to believe he was better than someone who merely worked for a living.

After this, he started to commit crimes. He would arrive at a person's apartment, knock on the door, and pretend to be a municipal engineer working for the city. He would say that he needed to come in and check out something. He had scoped out the apartment first, watching it to ensure that only a single woman lived there. Once he entered the apartment, he would murder and rob his victims.

In a matter of two weeks, Andrei was

responsible for committing five attacks on women in their apartments, robbing them all, and murdering two of them.

Andrei saw that his crimes were aired on a popular television show of the day, which made him excited and proud. He should have been scared of the publicity. But it had the opposite effect. His ego got so big that he decided to send the police a demand letter asking for the sum of fifty thousand rubles for him to stop the attacks. He never gave a return address for an answer. Instead, he told them to answer him on television.

The police agreed to play along. They said they would pay Andrei and give him the money at a railway station.

Dressed up like a construction worker on his way to work, Andrei walked by the police car that contained the money, quickly grabbed it and ran across the railway tracks and down into a basement door of a business. Police promptly followed him and blocked off the basement door. While in the basement, Andrei had a change of clothes stashed there, and he changed to look like someone different. Then he snuck upstairs into the business and slowly left out the front door with the money. Luckily, just outside the main door, a policeman was waiting, and he was arrested and taken to the police station for questioning.

Police searched Andrei's apartment and found several stolen items. He confessed almost immediately. He was charged with three murders and three attempted murders, convicted on all counts, and sentenced to death. He was executed by firing squad on August 5, 1991.

THIRTY-SIX

Sergey Maduev

THIEF OUTSIDE THE LAW

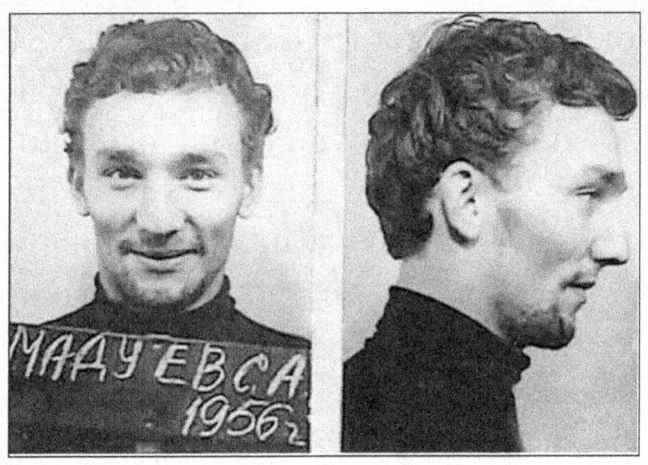

S ergey Maduev was born in the Karaganda prison in Kazakh, USSR, on June 17, 1956. He was the fourth child born to a Chechen prisoner who had been convicted for avoiding and resisting deportation. Once Sergey's father was released from jail, he abandoned him and his siblings. Sergey was forced to steal food to survive on the streets by the time he was six years old. In 1974, he was arrested and sent to jail, where he was sentenced to a six-year term for theft.

He served all six years of his sentence and was released in 1980. Sergey continued to survive by robbing people and apartments. He was arrested again in February 1981 and, this time, sentenced to serve fifteen years in prison.

In 1988, Sergey was transferred to a minimum security prison as he had had seven years of good behavior. Once he got to the new jail, he escaped. He then began a series of thefts throughout the country, constantly moving from place to place. His victims stated that Sergey was a mannerly thief because he didn't want to hurt his victims. One story told was of him going to the pharmacy to get medicine for one of his victims who was ill during the robbery. Another story claimed that when his accomplish tried to rape one of the victims, Sergey stopped it from happening.

But as time went by, Sergey began to kill his victims. When he was in Rostov with his accomplice, Roman Chemyshev, they were robbing a house. The couple who lived in the house were trying to escape by making enough noise to attract the attention of their neighbors. He then tied them up. After getting everything they wanted, they lit the house on fire. The couple and their one-year-old child all burned to death in the fire.

Investigators found that one of the adult victims was also shot in the head. The bullet was examined and found to have come from a rare gun in the Soviet Union. Some witnesses said that they saw a white Volga vehicle parked in their driveway on the night of the robbery and fire.

Detectives located that white car and talked to the owner, who said he had lent his car to his brother-in-law, Sergey. The police soon had a warrant out for his arrest.

Sergey and his accomplices were on the move. Next, they committed a double murder on June 6, 1989, while they were in the town of Astrakhan. They then traveled to Uzbek, where they stole over two hundred thousand rubles from other thieves. They fled to Leningrad, where they continued to commit robberies of people, businesses, and apartments. They killed two more people while there.

In 1990, they were doing another robbery in Tashkent. This time, it turned into a gunfight. Both the homeowner and Sergey's accomplice were killed, and Sergey himself was wounded. The following day, he was arrested at the railway station while trying to flee the town.

Sergey was convicted of two murders and sentenced to death on July 10, 1995, but because the death sentence moratorium was introduced, his sentence was reduced to life imprisonment. In December 2000, he died in prison of a heart attack.

THIRTY-SEVEN

Valery Asratyan

THE DIRECTOR

Valery Georgievich Asratyan was born in Yerevan, Armenia, USSR, sometime in 1958. His parents were Armenian and considered wealthy by the Soviet standard. His upbringing seemed quite good, with no issues.

But when Valery began school, he often wanted to play "doctor" with the girls. He would pretend to be a doctor and ask girls to undress so that he could examine his patients.

By the time Valery turned thirteen years old, he was having sex with a twenty-eight-year-old woman. After graduating in 1975, Valery studied psychology at the Armenian State University. While in college, he started to read many popular books. One of them was "Lolita," written by Vladimir Nabokov, where the main character, Humbert, was in a sexual relationship with a young girl. He believed himself to be like Humbert and often fantasized about the events in the book.

Valery graduated with a psychology degree in 1980 and got a job at a school teaching children with disabilities such as polio and cerebral palsy. Shortly after starting his career in 1981, he married a woman he had met in Moscow. After they wed, he decided to move to Moscow and into her place. This is about the time when Valery started committing crimes of a sexual nature with young girls. During his second attack on a young girl, he was caught and sent to a penal colony for two years. He was released in 1984, and within one year, he raped another young girl. He was caught, convicted, and imprisoned for two more years.

Again, Valery was released in 1987, and when he returned home, his wife kicked him out of their house and got a divorce. At first, he moved to Valuyki, Belgorod, to live briefly, but eventually, he decided to move back to Moscow. Upon his return, he met a divorced woman with a fourteen-year-old daughter and moved in with them.

Valery started committing his crimes again, but only this time, his girlfriend and daughter, whom he now lived with, would help him. He had started using drugs on his victims, such as tranquilizers and antipsychotics.

In early 1988, Valery pretended to be a film director and invited girls to his apartment to do a screen test. He would drug them, and when the girl lost consciousness, he would rape her for hours and steal the money and anything worth something from her before taking her to a train station on the outskirts of Moscow and leaving her there. When the victim was found, they couldn't remember anything because of the drugs that were given to her.

Over the next two years, he committed at least twelve rapes in this same manner.

Valery was taking some of the drugs himself,

which began to make him paranoid. He worried so much about being caught that he decided to kill his victims instead of letting them go.

What Valery feared the most would happen came true in 1990 when one of his surviving victims remembered what he did to her and was able to go to the police and report it. She was able to take detectives to where he had met with her and where he took her to assault her sexually.

Police used an undercover policewoman to act like a younger girl looking to be a model. She hung out in the area where he would cruise for the girls and took her to his place for a screen test. Eventually, he was caught and arrested.

In Sergey's first police interview, he confessed to having committed two murders and seventeen rapes. He became fearful of either being sentenced to death or being put in prison as a known child rapist. He knew he would probably be raped and attacked by other cellmates – the usual fate of criminals like him.

Valery was convicted of the two murders and seventeen rapes and sentenced to death. In 1996, he was executed in the Butyrku Prison by a firing squad.

THIRTY-EIGHT

Dmitry Gridin

THE LAST MANIAC OF THE USSR

Gridin was born in Magnitogorsk, Chelyabinsk, on March 4, 1968. His father was in charge of the Magnitogorsk Iron and Steel Works and was very popular in the community. They lived well above the expected standard of living in the USSR then. Not much is recorded about Dmitry's childhood or schooling, but as an adult, he went to the University of Magnitogorsk and was married with six children.

In the Summer of 1989, Gridin was walking down a street of houses when he spotted Zhana Terenchuk, a sixteen-year-old student sitting on the front porch of her home. He walked up her front stairs and strangled her to death, then left. That Summer, he attempted to do the same thing to three other girls, but all of them survived the attack. The police were able to get a good description of the attacker from the survivors.

As the Fall approached, Gridin attacked two more girls, Danzili Usmanova and Lyudmila Pozdnyakova. In both cases, he carelessly left his fingerprints. On November 25th, he attacked another woman on her porch, but she was much stronger than the other girls he had attacked and was able to fight him off. He fled, and when he did, he dropped his glasses and hat. When he was arrested later that day, he still had a knife on him.

There was so much anger in the town that people were demanding him to be executed in public. The trial began in the Fall of 1990. Within a month, his trial was over, and he was convicted of three murders and sentenced to death, but as the death penalty had just been stopped in the country, he was to serve out the rest of his life in prison.

Gridin is still alive and in prison today. He has applied for appeals to different crimes throughout jail, but every one of them has been rejected.

THIRTY-NINE

Vyacheslav Markin

THE SNUFFBOX DEVIL

Vyacheslav Vasilievich Markin was born in Leningrad sometime in 1948. He grew up living in a group or communal home. He never knew who his father was and didn't like his mother. As a child in school, he was disruptive and often stole other people's things. He had no friends or classmates with whom he hung around.

The first known theft was when Markin was heading to class and passed by an empty classroom with an open door. He saw a purse sitting on a desk. He entered the class, went through the purse, and found a wallet with one hundred and twenty rubles. He took it, brought it home, hid it, and returned to school. Later that same day, once the teacher realized that her wallet had been stolen, she called police. They came to the school and made a report, but the wallet was never found. This excited Markin because he got away with the theft.

A month later, Markin committed another theft. This time, he got away with one hundred and twenty rubles. Instead of keeping the money, he gave it to his mother, who never asked where he got it. In return, she bought him a brand-new bike.

Eventually, Markin was tired of living with his mother and attending school, so he ran away from home. He never stayed around town, either. He traveled from town to town with no destination in mind. He tried pickpocketing wallets and jewelry but was often caught. He was frequently sent to a home for misbehaving children, but he always escaped.

Markin decided he would do better stealing from people's homes. On one occasion, while he was robbing a house, the woman of the house returned home. He tied her up, beat and raped her before leaving. He was caught and arrested, and this time, he was given a fourteen-year sentence in prison.

After his release from prison, he went to the city of Skopin. A prisoner who had served time with him had lived there and told him he could come and stay with him when he got out. He met and started dating a divorced woman. He told her that he had been convicted and sent to prison but that he was innocent. She believed him and eventually married him.

Once they got an apartment together, he left, telling her he had to go on a business trip for work. But instead of working, he was robbing apartments and stealing people's money and valuables. He sold the stolen property and brought the money home to her. Soon, she became pregnant.

In 1990, while he was in Moscow robbing another apartment, he was caught in the act twice by the homeowners. In both cases, he overpowered them, beat them, and tied them up before leaving. Both victims survived their attacks.

Markin's first known murder happened when he was walking down a street with the ex-cellmate that he lived with for a while. They were looking for a place to rob. While walking, they ran into another of their old cellmates, Ryaby Ryabchikov, who hated Markin. They all got into a fight, and Markin ended up murdering Ryaby. He and his friend took Ryaby's body and dumped it off of a nearby railway embankment. Getting away with this murder seemed to give Markin the confidence he needed to kill others, as it was much easier to do than he thought.

Markin continued to rob people's homes, but now, anytime one of the owners came home, he wouldn't just tie them up. He would kill them instead. His next murder was when he was robbing an apartment. The landlady of the building knew that the tenant was away, so when she heard a noise coming from the apartment, she decided to go and look. There, she ran into Markin, and he strangled her to death.

Markin then decided to rob the neighbor of his wife's mother. He realized that some of the family was still home only after he crawled through their windows and entered the house. He killed all three of the people he found there: a mother, child, and grandmother. He raped the mother before killing her. When he was finished, he set the house on fire.

When police were investigating the triple murder, they noticed that the neighbors had a swing set out in their backyard. The swings were all tied with a unique sea knot, the same type of knot many of the victims had been tied with. After talking with Markin's mother-in-law, they went to speak with Markin himself.

While at Markin's place, they found several of the stolen items and seized them. They arrested Markin, who remained silent for a while. But he eventually confessed to everything once he saw all the evidence they had against him.

He was charged with six murders and several robberies and thefts. Before he could face trial, Markin hanged himself in his jail cell.

Sources

1. А.И. Ракитин. "Социализм не порождает преступности..." www.murders.ru.
2. A. Rakitin: *Socialism does not breed crime*. ISBN 978-5-7525-3028-9. ISBN 978-5-4490-2254-7.
3. The documentary film *Hellraiser* from the series *Legends of Soviet Investigation*.
4. Clarkson, Wensley (2021): *Serial Killers of Russia: Case Files from the World's Deadliest Nation*. London: Welbeck Publishing. ISBN 978-1-787-39602-9.
5. Conradi, Peter: *The Red Ripper: Inside the Mind of Russia's Most Brutal Serial Killer*. 1994. London. ISBN 0-440-21603-6
6. Cullen, Robert (1994): *The Killer Department*. ISBN: 1-85797-210-4
7. Hall, Susan (2020): *The World Encyclopedia of Serial Killers: Volume Three*, M–S. Denver, Colorado: WildBlue Press. ISBN 978-1-952-22533-8.
8. Lane, Brian (1994) [1991]: *The Butchers: A Casebook of Macabre Crimes and Forensic Detection*. Kettering: Index. ISBN 978-1-852-27297-5.
9. Matthews, Owen: *Moscow Times Newspaper*. January 30, 1999. "A Killer's Confidante In a Murderous Town"
10. *Legends of Soviet Investigation* – Steel Fingers Documentary film
11. Силач убийца (mzk2.ru)
12. T.V. Series: *Investigation Led* "Bloody Casanova."
13. Уткин, Анатолий Викторович". www.serial-killers.ru.

14. "On the trail of the "Vnukov" maniac" (petrovka-38.com)

15. Saratov Maniacs: Myths and Reality Saratovnews.ru (archive. ph)

16. Leonid Kanevsky: NTV "The Saratov maniac became the hero of the T.V. show" 19.02.2017. Saratov - BezFormata (archive.ph)

17. Маньяк Андрей Евсеев (mzk2.ru)

18. Nikolai Shestakov as Maniac (cumir.ru)

19. Good Aleksandrov: News archive

20. A film about the Iskitim maniac is being shot in Novosibirsk (archive. ph)

21. "The story of a serial maniac who killed an Omsk woman and burned her at the stake will be shown in a popular TV show" *SuperOmsk* (archive. ph)

22. "I Was Like a Predator on a Hunt" Interrogation Protocol of Maniac Fyodor Kozlov | VN.RU (archive. ph)

23. Фёдор Ибатович Раззаков [in Russian] (2008). Бандиты семидесятых, 1970—1979. Эксмо. pp. 370–371. ISBN 978-5699271429.

24. Condemn the "Ripper" | Newspaper "Nasha Vologda" (archive.ph)

25. Arinin V. Sakharov's Case, or Vologda Chikatilo (booksite.ru)

26. Охотник, переполошивший страну: Как примерный дружинник стал одним из самых безумных советских маньяков (life.ru)

27. Maniac Vasily Smirnov: From "Vasi the Cat" to "Gatchina Necromancer" Politics in Russia (politika-v-rashke.ru)

28. "Crimes and punishment of the Kursk maniac" (dddkursk.ru)

29. Fefilov, Nikolay Borisovich (serial-killers.ru)

30. In the Urals, searching for a serial maniac-KP.RU.
31. Peter Onradi: *The Red Ripper: Inside the Mind of Russia's Most Brutal Serial Killer*. ISBN 0-86369-618-X. 1992
32. Robert Cullen: *Detective Viktor Burakov's Eight-Year Hunt*. ISBN 1-85797-210-4 1993
33. Krivich, Mikhail: *Comrade Chikatilo: The Psychopathology of Russia's Notorious Serial Killer*. Barricade Books. ISBN 0-942-63790-9.1993
34. Richard Lourie: *Hunting the Devil*. HarperCollins. ISBN 0-586-21846-7. 1993
35. Maniac Kulik: *Helped to Catch Rostov Maniac Chikatilo: History of Irkutsk Militia* (archive.org)
36. Vasyl Kulik (bbok.ru)
37. "Marginal Kamensky maniac Igor Cernat" Criminal investigation. Petrograd. Leningrad – St. Petersburg
38. U.S. News in Russian Language Online Today: Read Watch U.S. News in Russian Language, R.Reklama Newspaper (rusrek.com)
39. "How not to become a victim of a maniac?" Highlights from April 16, 2004, Archive of the website of the publishing house "Severnaya Nedelya" (vdvsn.ru)
40. "Black tights turned him on," who was killed by the Taganrog maniac Tsyuman, RIA Novosti, 25.07.2020
41. "The Last Bandit of the Soviet Union" (sovsekretno.ru)
42. "Maniac Golovkin was shot in front of me – A lifer remembered the death penalty" MK
43. Supreme Court of the Russian Federation (archive.org)

44. "The last maniac of the USSR" was denied parole. Magnitogorsk "lifter" will remain behind bars | Verstov.Info

45. The documentary film *The Last Knot* from the series *Criminal Russia*

About the Author

Alan R Warren is a Bestselling Author, Producer, and host of the popular NBC Radioshow *House of Mystery* and *Inside Writing*, both heard on the 106.5 F.M. Los Angeles/102.3 F.M. Riverside/ 1050 A.M. Palm Springs/ 540 A.M. KYAH Salt Lake City/  1150 A.M. KKNW Seattle/Tacoma and Phoenix.

His bestselling true crime books in Canada include *Beyond Suspicion: The True Story of Colonel Russell Williams*, which will be featured on CNN's *Lies, Crimes, & Videos* (Season 4), and *Murder Times Six: The True Story of the Wells Gray Park Murders*. In America, his bestsellers include *The Killing Game: Serial Killer Rodney Alcala*, which was featured on several television shows such as *Very Scary People with Donny Walberg*, Oxygen's *Mark of a Killer*, Reelz' *Killer Trophies*, and soon to be included in a four-part Sundance Channel documentary called *Death's Date*. His bestseller, *Doomsday Cults: The Devil's Hostages*, was featured on Vice's *Dark Side of the '90s*.

His latest series, *Killer Queens*, is a six-part book series covering murders that affect the Gay Community. So far, it includes Book 1 - Leopold & Loeb, Book 2 - Butcher of Hanover: Fritz Haarmann, Book 3 - Grindr Serial Killer: Stephen Port, and Book 4 - Bruce McArthur: Toronto Gay Killer.

Also By Alan R. Warren

Beyond Suspicion: Russell Williams – A Canadian Serial Killer

Young girl's panties started to go missing; sexual assaults began to occur, and then female bodies were found! Soon this quiet town of Tweed, Ontario, was in a panic. What is even more shocking was when an upstanding resident stood accused of the assaults. This was not just any man, but a pillar of the community; a decorated military pilot who had flown Canadian Forces VIP aircraft for dignitaries such as the Queen of England, Prince Philip, the Governor-General and Prime Minister of Canada.

This is the story of serial killer Russell Williams, the elite pilot of Canada's Air Force One, and the innocent victims he murdered. Unlike other serial killers, Williams seemed very unaffected about his crimes and leading two different lives.

Alan R. Warren describes the secret life including the

abductions, rape, and murders that were unleashed on an unsuspecting community. Included are letters written to the victims by Williams and descriptions of the assaults and rapes as seen on videos and photos taken by Williams during the attacks.

This updated version also contains the full brilliant police interrogation of Williams and his confession. Also, the twisted way the Williams planned to pin his crimes on his unsuspecting neighbor.

Doomsday Cults: The Devil's Hostages

Jim Jones convinced his 1000 followers they would all have to commit suicide since he was going to die. Shoko Asahara convinced his followers to release a weapon of mass destruction, the deadly sarin gas, on a Tokyo subway. The Order of the Solar Temple lured the rich and famous, including Princess Grace of Monaco, and convinced them to die a fiery death now on Earth to be reborn on a better planet called Sirius. Charles Manson convinced his followers to kill, in an attempt to incite an apocalyptic race war.

These are a few of the doomsday cults examined in this

book by bestselling author Alan R. Warren. Its focus is on cults whose destructive behavior was due in large part to their apocalyptic beliefs or doomsday movements. It includes details surrounding the massacres and a look into how their members became so brainwashed they committed unimaginable crimes at the command of their leader.

Usually, when we hear about these cults and their massacres, we ask ourselves how it possibly happened. We could also ask ourselves, what then is the difference between a cult and a religion? We once had a small group of people who unquestionably followed a person who believed he was the son of God. Two thousand years later, that following is one of the most recognized religions in the world. This book in no way criticizes believing in God. Rather, it examines how a social movement grows into a full religion and when it does not. And what makes the conventional faiths such as Christianity, Judaism, Islam, and Hinduism stand above groups such as the Branch Davidians or Children of God.

In Chains: The Dangerous World of Human Trafficking

Human trafficking is the trade of people for forced labor or sex. It also includes the illegal extraction of human organs and tissues. And it is an extremely ruthless and dangerous industry plaguing our world today.

Most believe human trafficking occurs in countries with no human rights legislation. This is a myth. All types of human trafficking are alive and well in most of the developed countries of the world like the United States, Canada, and the UK. It is estimated that $150 billion a year is generated in the forced labor industry alone. It is also believed that 21 million

people are trapped in modern-day slavery – exploited for sex, labor, or organs.

Most also believe since they live in a free country, there is built-in protection against such illegal practices. But for many, this is not the case. Traffickers tend to focus on the most vulnerable in our society, but trafficking can happen to anyone. You will see how easy it can happen in the stories included in "In Chains."

BUTCHER OF HANOVER: Fritz Haarmann (Killer Queens 2)

Killer Queens is a new series of historical fiction books based on true stories. Sources, such as police reports and newspaper articles, are examined to gather as many facts as possible surrounding each case. As with any work of fiction, some creative additions are made when

BUTCHER
of HANOVER

FRITZ HAARMANN

Book 2: Killer Queens

ALAN R. WARREN
Bestselling Author

Foreword by Mike Browne

telling these stories, usually within the conversations between the personalities involved. The various sources are the basis of these conversations and hopefully, make them come alive for the readers to help understand what was meant by those words.

Book 2 of the series focuses on the serial killer of at least twenty-seven young men and boys in Germany in the post-World War I era. At the center of this murder case were Fritz Haarmann and Hans Grans, who were lovers while committing these murders. It wasn't until the skulls and bones started washing ashore from the Leine River in Hanover that Germany realized they had a cold-blooded serial killer in their country.

Unlike Leopold and Loeb murder case covered in Book 1, where the dominance shifted from one to the other, Fritz Haarmann was the dominant partner in this case. He carried out each of the murders and dismemberment of the bodies himself, even though he claimed that Grans chose who was to be murdered in court.

As you read the exploration of the case in this book, ask yourself, did Haarmann murder each victim to keep his lover Hans Grans to stay with him? Did Grans decide who it was that was to be murdered? The evidence on this case will keep you on the edge of your seat, trying to determine who was really behind these gruesome murders.

MURDER TIMES SIX: The True Story of The Wells Park Murders

"The author even had me (who conducted the interview) on the edge of my seat as I was turning the pages as "the Detective" was trying to unearth the unspeakable truth."

Sgt. Mike Eastham R.C.M.P.

It was a crime unlike anything seen in British Columbia. The horror of the "Wells Gray Murders" almost forty years ago transcends decades.

On August 2, 1982, three generations of a family set out on a camping trip – Bob and Jackie Johnson, their two daughters, Janet, 13 and Karen, 11, and Jackie's parents, George and Edith Bentley. A month later, the Johnson family car was found off a mountainside logging road near Wells Gray Park completely burned out. In the back seat were the incinerated remains of four adults, and in the trunk were the two girls.

But this was not just your average mass murder. It was much worse. Over time, some brutal details were revealed; however, most are still only known to the murderer, David Ennis (formerly Shearing). His crimes had far-reaching impacts on the family, community, and country. It still does today. Every time Shearing attempts freedom from the parole board, the grief is triggered as everyone is forced to relive the horrors once again.

Murder Times Six shines a spotlight on the crime that captured the attention of a nation, recounts the narrative of a complex police investigation, and discusses whether a convicted mass murderer should ever be allowed to leave the confines of an institution. Most importantly, it tells the story of one family forever changed.

www.ingramcontent.com/pod-product-compliance
Lightning Source LLC
Chambersburg PA
CBHW070916120626
46546CB00001B/292